His Guilt

Center Point
Large Print

Books are
produced in the
United States
using U.S.-based
materials

Books are printed
using a revolutionary
new process called
THINKtech™ that
lowers energy usage
by 70% and increases
overall quality

Books are
durable and
flexible
because of
smythe-sewing

Paper is
sourced using
environmentally
responsible
foresting methods
and the
paper is acid-free

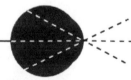

**This Large Print Book carries the
Seal of Approval of N.A.V.H.**

His Guilt

The Amish of Hart County

Shelley Shepard Gray

CENTER POINT LARGE PRINT
THORNDIKE, MAINE

This Center Point Large Print edition
is published in the year 2017 by arrangement with
Avon Inspire, an imprint of HarperCollins Publishers.

The text of this Large Print edition is unabridged.
In other aspects, this book may vary
from the original edition.
Printed in the United States of America
on permanent paper.
Set in 16-point Times New Roman type.

ISBN: 978-1-68324-475-2

Library of Congress Cataloging-in-Publication Data

Names: Gray, Shelley Shepard, author.
Title: His guilt : the Amish of Hart County / Shelley Shepard Gray.
Description: Center Point Large Print edition. | Thorndike, Maine :
    Center Point Large Print, 2017.
Identifiers: LCCN 2017021928 | ISBN 9781683244752
    (hardcover : alk. paper)
Subjects: LCSH: Amish—Fiction. | Large type books. | GSAFD:
    Mystery fiction.
Classification: LCC PS3607.R3966 H57 2017 | DDC 813/.6—dc23
LC record available at https://lccn.loc.gov/2017021928

To Laurie Smith.
Thank you for inspiring me in more ways than you can imagine! You are a blessing to me.

Greater love has no one than this: to lay down one's life for one's friends.

JOHN 15:13 (NIV)

Whatever your past has been, you have a spotless future.

AMISH PROVERB

Chapter 1

Horse Cave, Kentucky
August 4

He was watching her again.

As she handed her customer change across the counter of the Blooms and Berries nursery, Waneta Cain did her best to pretend that their newest employee was not inordinately interested in everything she did. He was simply observant.

Surely, it was just her imagination playing tricks on her anyway. Mark Fisher was probably trying to see how she handled the checkout counter. She used to watch Mr. Lehmann all the time when she'd first started at the nursery.

That had to be the reason.

"Thanks for your help, Neeta," Mr. Killian said, interrupting her thoughts. "I'd be lost without you."

"I'm simply glad I could help ya," she told the Englisher with a bright smile as he lifted his box of seedlings from the wide well-worn countertop. "See ya soon."

The man tipped his ball cap. "You sure will

if I can't get these to bear fruit. Wish me luck."

"Good luck and good blessings, too." After helping him with the door, she let it close behind her with a satisfying *thunk*.

She chuckled to herself. That Mr. Killian was a terrible gardener but a frequent customer. She sincerely hoped that one day he would develop that green thumb he wanted so badly.

"Do you always act that way?"

A shiver coursed through her as she turned.

Meeting Mark's dark-brown eyes, which seemed to be studying her intently, she struggled to appear calm. "Like what?"

Mark stepped away from the row of metal shelves located in the back of the store. He'd been unpacking boxes and restocking shelves for the last hour. Methodically sorting and organizing merchandise while she helped customers. "Like they're your friends," he replied. "Like you're so happy to see them." Stepping closer, he lifted a shoulder. "Is that how you really are . . . or is that just an act?"

She didn't care for the way he seemed to be insinuating that she wasn't genuine. "It's not an act. Mr. Killian is in here a lot. He's nice. We are friends."

"He's English and must be fifty years old."

"I don't see how that matters. I can like people who are different than me."

"Maybe you can. But you were sure smiling at

him a lot. Or do you do that on purpose? To make sure that he will return?"

His question made her uncomfortable, but his sarcastic tone made her angry. "I don't know why you are asking such things. I really don't like what you are suggesting. I'm not doing anything out of the ordinary or smiling at customers in any special way. I'm just being my regular self."

"Huh. So you treat everyone with smiles and kindness. You are friends with all sorts of people. Even people who are different from you. Except me."

"I've been perfectly amiable to you," she retorted. Except, of course, that was a lie.

"I don't think so," Mark murmured. "I've been here seven hours, four of them barely six feet away from you."

She knew that. She'd known exactly where he was every moment that they'd been together. "And?"

"And during all that time you've hardly said ten words to me. You sure aren't smiling at *me*."

She opened her mouth, closed it again. What could she say? He wasn't wrong.

Mark stepped closer, invading her space. She could see the fine brown hairs on his forearms now. Noticed that he hadn't shaved in a day or two.

"Is it because I was once taken in for questioning?" he asked quietly, his dark-brown eyes watching her, as if he feared she would run.

9

"Or, is it just me? Do you not want anything to do with me, Waneta?"

Her palms were sweating. She fisted both as she tried to come up with an answer. He was right on all accounts. She was uneasy around him.

Fact was, Mark Fisher was a large man. Tall and well-muscled. He had a rough way about him, too. It was disconcerting.

Of course, she'd always felt uneasy around him. He'd been an angry teenager, always glaring and short-tempered with most everyone. After he finished school, he'd worked for a few people around town. Rumor had it that his brother, Calvin, had taken off soon after their mother did. Mark had even lived in Mr. Lehmann's home for a time, until he was taken in for questioning about Bethany's assault.

And after he was questioned, then let go for insufficient evidence, he disappeared for two years.

Now he was back.

Mr. Lehmann assured her that Mark hadn't done anything wrong, but a lot of people in the community still believed that he was the masked man who'd beaten Bethany Williams. It wasn't much of a stretch. Bethany had told lots of people that her assailant was over six feet tall and was very strong. But she also said that she wasn't able to identify the man.

Few other details had circulated after that. Then Bethany and her family moved up north, practically the moment she was released from the hospital.

Realizing Mark was still waiting, Waneta said, "I haven't spoken to you much because we don't know each other."

His eyes narrowed. "But that's not really true. We knew each other once. We did go to the same Amish school."

"You were ahead of me in school. We hardly talked then." He was only three years older than herself, but they were miles apart in terms of how they'd lived their lives. He'd also been the kind of boy she'd been a little scared of. He was rough and had always seemed so angry.

For a second, he looked dumbfounded. "So, you do remember."

"Of course I remember you and your brother, Calvin. Our school wasn't that big, Mark." Feeling pretty good about how self-assured she was sounding, Neeta folded her arms across her chest. "But that was a long time ago. Years have gone by."

"Yeah. You're right," he said slowly. "Years *have* gone by. Practically a whole lifetime."

He sounded so sad. She wondered what was going through his head. Did he regret hurting Bethany? And what had he been doing for the two years since it all had happened? Why had he even come back to Horse Cave? Surely, there were other, far better places to start over.

The door jangled as a couple came in. Like Mr. Killian, they were regular customers. James and Katie Eicher were Amish and lived on a large farm on the outskirts of town.

Glad for the reprieve, she smiled at them. "Hiya, Katie. James. How can I help you?"

Just as Katie was about to answer, her husband put a hand on her arm. "Go wait in the buggy, Kate."

Katie looked at her husband in confusion, then blanched when she caught sight of Mark. Without a word, she turned and walked back out the door.

When it closed again, James glared at Mark. "What are you doing here?"

Mark lifted his chin. "I work here."

"Is that true, Neeta?" James asked. "Did Henry actually hire him?"

"*Jah.* Today is Mark's first day." Unsure how to handle his anger, she cleared her throat. "Now, um, how may I help you?"

"Where is Henry?"

She looked around the room, which was a ridiculous exercise, seeing as it was perfectly obvious that Mr. Lehmann was not there.

"He's out back," Mark said, pointing to one of the four large greenhouses behind the retail store. "You want me to go get him for ya?"

"I don't want you to do a thing for me," James said. "I'll go find him myself."

Mark rocked back on his heels. "Suit yourself."

Neeta winced at his flippant tone.

James, however, looked irate. Pointing a finger at him, James said, "I'm telling you now, Fisher. You stay far away from my wife. Don't talk to her. Don't even look at her."

Instead of looking cowed, the corners of Mark's lips lifted. "Or what?"

"Or I'll do everything I can to ensure that you leave here for good."

Mark narrowed his eyes. "Are you threatening me?"

Ignoring Mark again, James turned to her. "I can't believe you are working in here with him. Do your parents even know?"

Before she could say that they did not, James strode out the door. It slammed in his wake.

For a good couple of seconds, Neeta stared at the door. She tried to calm herself, especially since she'd just realized that her hands were shaking.

Why was she so rattled? Was it because she was afraid of Mark Fisher?

Or because James's anger had been so scorching?

"You never answered him," Mark said from behind her, startling her out of her dark thoughts. "Do your parents know that you are working here with me?"

"*Nee.*"

"Why not?" he asked. "Is it because you're afraid that they'll want you to you stay far, far away from the dangerous Mark Fisher, too?"

Before she could answer, the door opened again. This time it brought in Mr. Lehmann.

He looked from Mark to her and sighed. "I came to check on how you two are doing after James Eicher's visit. It don't look like you're doing too *gut*."

"I'm fine, Mr. Lehmann," she said. "But, um, well, it's four o'clock."

"Which means it's time for you to get on home," he said with a kind smile. "Grab your things and get on your way. We'll see you tomorrow."

She smiled weakly as she turned toward the back storage room, where her belongings were stowed. For the first time since she'd started working at the nursery, returning to work filled her with dread.

She didn't trust Mark. Worse, she didn't trust herself when she was around him.

Chapter 2

August 4

Mark exhaled as he watched Waneta Cain hop on her bicycle and ride down the driveway toward the main road that led into Horse Cave.

What was wrong with him? He'd been nothing but rude to her all day. He'd been so direct and angry, it was like he'd been picking a fight. Why had he acted that way?

After Henry turned the Open sign to Closed and locked the front door, he walked to Mark's side. "Care to tell me what's been going on between the two of you?"

"Not really." When Henry crossed his arms over his chest, obviously ready to stand and glare at him until he got the explanation he'd asked for, Mark dared to tell the truth. "All right. I'm pretty sure she's scared of me."

"Scared might be putting things a bit harsh, son."

As it always did, Henry's use of *son* eased him like little else did. Henry Lehmann was the only person Mark trusted.

He was also the only person with whom he

could let down his guard. From the time Mark was old enough to care, Henry had believed in his worth, even when his parents hardly knew he existed. Even when his teacher looked at him warily, like he was about to steal something off the top of her desk.

Henry had also taught him about love and kindness. About steadfastness and loyalty, too. For that, Mark tried his best to give the sixty-year-old man honesty, even when it hurt to be so vulnerable.

"Scared might be harsh, but it's accurate," Mark said. "I meant to act better, I tried to act better, but after Waneta hardly looked at me for most of the day, something snapped. I said a lot of things I shouldn't have."

"Sounds like the both of you had a difficult day, then."

"No worse than you. My being here cost you customers, didn't it?"

Henry walked to the counter, opened the cash box, and started counting the bills. "If you're talking about James Eicher, it ain't no great loss. He doesn't come in that much anyway."

There was his answer. His presence was costing Henry money and that was no way to repay him for the job. Mark's pride told him that he should quit, not burden the best man he'd ever known. And certainly not take out his frustrations and anger on a sweet, nice woman like Waneta Cain.

But he had no other options for employment.

No one else had wanted to hire him, and Mark had asked most everyone in the area. He needed employment and he needed the money it gave him if he was going to follow through on his goal of living in his old house and fixing it up into something special.

Henry squeezed his shoulder. "Stop fretting, Mark. I'm sure you didn't say anything to Neeta that canna be soothed with an apology. Waneta is a nice girl with a fine heart. She'll come around. Other folks will, too. It just takes time."

He hoped Henry was right. "I'll try harder tomorrow."

"I reckon you're trying hard enough. Just relax and settle in. Once you show Neeta the real you, she'll like you fine. In no time, the two of you will be getting along like salt and pepper."

"You make that sound so easy."

Compassion filled the older man's light-blue eyes. "I suppose it won't be easy. But remember this. I'm not going to fire you."

"*Danke.*"

"I'm also not going to let you quit."

The older man looked like a bantam rooster, he was so fired up. "So you're saying that I've got no choice but to stick it out," Mark teased.

"None whatsoever," Henry replied with a trace of humor sparkling in his eyes. Handing Mark a silver ring of keys, he said, "Now, go out and lock up the greenhouses. Double-check that all the water hoses are turned off, too, if you please."

Taking the key ring, Mark exited the building and exhaled. The August sun was still burning bright in the sky, practically scorching the ground below. They really needed rain.

He rolled his shoulders, trying to ease the tense muscles around his neck. Maybe it was the weather that was making him so crazy. The ninety-degree heat, combined with the high humidity, was enough to make even the best of men feel out of sorts.

As he entered one greenhouse after another, he dutifully checked the hoses and picked up anything that he was sure was out of place. At the same time, he attempted to reconcile his reasons for returning to Horse Cave in the first place.

He hadn't had a good childhood here. His parents had been emotionally abusive and completely negligent. Though they were Amish, nothing about their way of life followed the *Ordnung*, the set of rules that governed everyday Amish life. Mark remembered the preacher or bishop visiting their home often.

After those visits, things would get better, then progressively get worse again. Looking back on those days, Mark knew his parents had done very little to help or provide for him or his younger brother, Calvin. He'd hated that. Had resented them, too. He and Calvin had been the hungry boys in the classroom. The ones with the dirty clothes and the homework never done.

As he'd gotten older, Mark tried his best to look after his brother, but his efforts were never good enough. By then, Calvin had changed. Gone was the hopeful boy who yearned for acceptance. In his place was someone who was conniving and desperate. He'd ignore Mark's efforts to get him to study, and spent most of his free time away from home.

Then, just when Mark thought their situation couldn't have gotten any worse, it did. One morning, after a particularly bad fight, he and Calvin woke up to their father sitting at the kitchen table alone. He informed them that their mother had left in the middle of the night, and she wasn't coming back.

When Calvin blamed their *daed*, their father hit him. Hard. Scared and fed up, his little brother left that day. He was barely fourteen.

From then on, it was just Mark and his father. Mark wasn't sure why he stayed. His father had been angry and emotionally abusive. He'd stopped working, stopped going to church. Eventually, he left the faith, and started being even more self-destructive.

Mark began taking odd jobs to help pay the bills and buy food. Henry Lehmann had always allowed him to work around the nursery, sweeping and cleaning the greenhouses and walkways on the property.

And though he kept going to church, and even met with the preacher, much of their community distanced themselves even further from him.

His brother's leaving had nearly broken him. His mother's departure, his father's abandonment of their faith and descent into drug use, had left him shocked. However, it was the church community's disregard for his needs that caused the most pain. He'd never felt more alone.

But it was being suspected of assaulting Bethany Williams that had shaken him to the core.

How had that happened? How was it possible that a girl in their community had gotten attacked? And how come Sheriff Brewer decided that Mark was the one who'd done it? He'd spent most of his life trying to do the right thing in the worst sort of circumstances. He finished school, tried to take care of his brother. He'd even tried to take care of his parents.

But after Bethany was assaulted, all that anyone seemed to remember was that he'd been the kid with the dirty clothes, messed-up family, and very little supervision.

The moment the charges were dropped and he was free to leave the area, Mark finally came to terms with the fact that Horse Cave held nothing for him. Not anymore. Maybe it never had. He headed to Indiana and got a job in an RV factory near the Illinois state line. The work had been good and Mark was able to save a lot of money.

While he was there, he was able to let down his guard some. The men he worked with thought he was just like them: a young Amish man trying to make something of himself. Only when he was sitting in his apartment late at night did he allow himself to think of his childhood in Horse Cave. He'd remember the windy, hilly roads, the creeks, the abundance of trees, and the scent of wildflowers in the air.

He'd lost track of Calvin and had pretended his father didn't exist. The only person he kept in contact with was Henry, and that was because Henry had refused to give up on him. Only when Henry informed him that the small house he'd grown up in was now his—and mentioned that his doctor had been cautioning him to cut back on his seventy-hour workweeks—did Mark decide to return.

So, here he was. Two years later, but it felt like everything he'd been running from had happened just yesterday.

After locking up the last greenhouse tight, Mark squinted at the sun. He was going to be in for a long night. There was no way he was going to be able to simply walk around his house, yet again, dodging memories of his father. Knowing that his father was gone forever, and that nothing between them had ever been resolved, was hard to swallow. He supposed he'd always held out a sliver of hope that his father would one day seek him out and ask for his forgiveness. But that had never happened.

So, going home right away was out.

Instead, he would walk over to the salvage market, pick up a couple of things in the sale aisle, and stop by the library. Or maybe he would go to Bill's Diner. He'd been avoiding that place, knowing he'd see a lot of people in the community there. But perhaps it was time.

"You got everything locked up tight?" Henry asked when Mark walked back inside.

"*Jah*," he replied as he handed Henry his keys. "Everything is locked and the hoses are all off. I checked each one like you asked me to."

"Would you like to join me for supper? I've got some leftovers from last night's taco casserole."

Henry was a huge fan of creating his own casseroles out of leftovers in his refrigerator. After choking down something called pork chop surprise, Mark had sworn never to eat another one of Henry's suppers again. "*Danke*, but I thought I might go to the diner. It's liver-and-onion night. Want to join me?"

Henry grimaced. "I'll pass, son. No matter how I've tried, I never could abide it. You enjoy your meal, though, and I'll see ya at eight tomorrow, right?"

Mark nodded. "I'll be here."

Henry peered over the rims of his glasses at him. "I'll be here, too, son. See you then."

Chapter 3

August 4

W hat do you think about going to Bill's tonight, Neeta?" her mother asked practically the moment Waneta walked in the back door. "They've got a mighty good special for supper. Liver and onions!"

It took everything she had not to grimace. "It's been an awfully long day, Mamm. I was hoping to stay here and relax."

"But Daed and I have been sitting here all day, practically just watching the hands on the clock move around. We were hoping to get out a bit."

"Oh, Mamm." Waneta hid a smile. Her mother might have been watching the clock, but Daed had most likely been far more interested in his new book or napping. After his last "episode"—which he seemed to have taken in stride, but which scared her mother and Waneta half to death—Daed was put on several new heart medicines, and they were taking a toll on him. Some days he seemed to be able to tolerate them just fine; other times, they didn't seem to agree with him at all. Except for his biweekly attendance at church, he rarely left the house anymore. He said his body simply preferred being comfortable in his easy chair.

Which was why Waneta knew that her father had definitely not been the clock-watcher parent that day. It had been her mother, who was still the most social member of their little family.

"Mamm, how did you find out it was liver-and-onion night at Bill's?"

"Ruth stopped by around three. She said she was going around five thirty, before the supper rush." Looking a little winsome, she added, "I believe Faith is going, too."

Her mother, Ruth, and Faith were best friends. As far as Waneta could surmise, they'd been best friends practically since birth. Ruth was married and lived just down the street; Faith's husband passed away almost five years ago.

All three had been new brides together and, later, new mothers. Still, whenever they got together, they acted like silly girls. They'd gossip and laugh, plan future meetings and work on sewing projects.

In short, they were lovely women. Devout and kind. Sweet and fun. But they also had the difficult habit of encouraging Neeta's *mamm* to do things that weren't possible—and rarely offering her a way to do them.

"Mamm, next time Ruth mentions that she's going out to supper, you ought to ask if you could go with her."

Her mother's eyes brightened, but she shook her head. "I couldn't leave your father," she whispered. Well, tried to whisper. Her mother had never really mastered that art.

"Sure, you could," Daed barked from his easy chair.

Waneta chuckled. "See?"

"But I don't want him to be lonely."

"He won't be lonely if you leave him for an hour or two to enjoy a meal with your friends at the diner, Mamm. He'll be okay. Plus, I'm home now. I'm going to have supper with him."

"You don't think we could get your father to go out to supper? It might be good for him."

"I'm fine, Gettie," he called out.

Waneta knew this was hard for her mother, this first time of leaving him home while she went out. However, she also knew that her mother was going to have to get used to doing things like this. Norman Cain's health wasn't going to get better; the doctors told the three of them that in no uncertain terms.

Gently, Waneta said, "You know Daed doesn't like to eat in public anymore. His hands shake. And he is tired by five or six each evening."

"But—"

"Mamm, like I said, I'm tired, too. I worked all day. I don't want to take Daed out to eat. I'm sorry."

Mamm swallowed hard. "Nothing to be sorry

about, dear. You are right. I shouldn't make such a fuss about such things anyway."

Making a decision, Neeta turned to the bench by the back door where her mother had set her purse for as long as she could remember. Picking it up, she handed it to her mother. "It's almost five thirty. I bet neither Ruth nor Faith has started walking to Bill's Diner yet. Go down and ask Ruth if you can walk with her."

Her eyes widened. "I couldn't do that! It is rude." But even as she said the words, she reached for her bag.

"It might be rude if you didn't know those women so well, but you know them practically better than me," Waneta teased. "Go on, Mamm. Go enjoy a nice supper out. I promise, Daed and I will be happy to relax together."

Though she was still clutching her black leather purse like a lifeline, her mother glanced into the living room. "Do you think he'll feel secretly sad that I'm leaving him?"

"I won't!" he called out.

"He's going to be as glad as I am that he's not eating liver and onions, Mamm. Go, now."

Her mother walked toward the door. "Maybe I'll bring you both some slices of pie."

"*Danke*. I will enjoy that. Pie will taste *gut*." Waneta made a shooing motion with her hands. "Say hello to Ruth and Faith for me!"

With a new set to her shoulders, Gettie walked out the door. Watching from the window, Waneta felt a lump form in her throat. This must have been what her mother felt when she had walked to school for the first time on her own. Waneta had felt both pride and a bit lost.

Change was hard.

When her mother was out of sight, Neeta went to check on her father. He had the paper opened on his lap, his reading glasses perched on his nose, and an amused expression on his face.

"That was quite an accomplishment there, daughter. I'm proud of you."

"You thought it was the right thing to do, too, *jah*?"

"Of course I did. Your mother worries too much."

"She loves you."

"I love her, too, which is why I'm pleased she got out of here for a bit. It's good for her."

"She'll have a nice time with Ruth and Faith."

He nodded. "I'll get a break, too. Your mother fusses over me all day long. Even when I'm sleeping." Looking mildly aggrieved, he added, "You know, she never has gotten the hang of whispering."

"Faith's daughter Grace once told me that her parents thought that Mamm would have made a great preacher, if women did such things. Her voice can sure carry."

27

"No one would ever sleep during her sermons. Ain't so?"

Perching on the chair next to him, she joked, "We might want to mention that to Preacher Eli next time he comes to call." Sharing a smile with him, she said, "Anyway, I'm glad Mamm went. She really loves liver and onions."

"Indeed, she does. But her going out wasn't about liver, child. It was about becoming a little bit more independent. It needed to be done." That smile was replaced by a look that was far more reflective. Maybe a little wistful, too. "It was time, don'tcha think?"

How could a question like that hurt so badly? Especially when she'd just been thinking the very same thing? Wordlessly, she nodded.

"What are you going to make me for supper, child?"

Even though she'd already told him, she said it again. "I thought I'd make some chicken, potatoes, and broccoli. Does that sound okay?"

"It sounds just fine, dear," he said as he closed his eyes. "Wake me up when it's ready."

Getting to her feet, Waneta walked to the kitchen, opened the refrigerator, and pulled out the package of chicken.

Around her, the house was dim and silent. Warm, even with the windows being open.

It was a summer evening. The kind, when she was a child, that she loved.

She'd loved spending the majority of each day in bare feet. Loved the feel of the sun on her skin; loved the air filled with the scent of freshly cut grass and her mother's roses.

But just like the seasons, her childhood had passed. She now had responsibilities and new worries. Things that only adults should worry about.

Things like her father's failing health, her mother's tentativeness about her looming independence. And, she supposed, her new coworker.

Why had God placed Mark in her life? What did He want her to do? Perhaps just as importantly, she needed to figure out what she wanted to do about him. Did she want to continue to keep him at a distance, doing her best to keep her conversation, and smiles, to a minimum? Or, did she need to grow up and remember that he deserved her compassion and kindness as much as anyone else in Hart County?

That was a lot to think about as she sliced potatoes and prepared the simple meal.

To her surprise, Waneta was still thinking about Mark when her mother came home, as she sat in her quiet room—and long after she would have been fast asleep. Unable to stop herself, she continually replayed their conversations in her head and wondered how she could have acted differently.

Suddenly, it all made sense. The Lord wanted

her to make amends. To change her attitude toward Mark. She shouldn't have acted so distant toward him. She should have talked to him more, looked him in the eye. She should've been a whole lot nicer.

That was why she hadn't been able to think about hardly anything else.

Tomorrow, she resolved to try harder to be his friend.

Chapter 4

Friday, August 5

Neeta, I didn't even tell you about the big news everyone was talking about last night," Mamm said as she slid two fried eggs onto Waneta's breakfast plate. Every morning without fail, her mother got up and fixed her a big breakfast. Just the way she had when she was a young girl.

Waneta couldn't count the number of times she'd told her mother that there was no need to do such a thing anymore. But it was now apparent that, while it might not be necessary for Waneta, her mother needed to feel like she was still doing something to take care of her, even if it was in this small way.

Taking the plate from her, Neeta added toast and a slice of sausage, then quickly closed her eyes and gave thanks. When she opened her eyes again, her mother was bringing her a fresh cup of coffee.

"Here you are, dear. Piping hot with two tea-spoons of sugar. Just the way you like it."

After taking a grateful sip, Waneta smiled. "I don't know how you do it, Mamm. Your *kaffi* always tastes better than mine."

Her mother beamed. "That's because someone else made it. Food made by other people always tastes better. That's why people go to restaurants."

"I think you may have a point, Mamm," she said with a laugh. "So, what was your big news? You look like you're about to burst."

Taking the chair next to Waneta, her mother's eyes lit up. "Mark Fisher was at the diner last night."

"Oh?" Quickly, Waneta took a bite of toast before she lost her appetite.

"Oh, yes. At first I wasn't sure who he was. But Ruth knew. She told me. And, she reminded me all about his attack on Bethany." Wrapping her palms around her own cup of coffee, her mother said, "I can't believe I had almost forgotten that. Why, I might have talked to him by accident!"

Never before had her mother's penchant for gossip bothered her like it did at that minute. It also made her uncomfortably aware just how judgmental she'd been at work the day before. "Mamm, Mark was proven innocent. He had nothing to do with Bethany getting beat up so badly. You shouldn't say such things."

"But don't you think the policemen got it

wrong? Everyone who Ruth and Faith and I talked to last night think so."

Waneta could just imagine the conversations that they had! "Oh, Mamm."

Ignoring her moan, Mamm continued. "Just so you know, I think other people in town doubt his innocence, too. No one besides Lora, his server, said a word to him the whole time he was there. And I'm sure she only did because she didn't have a choice."

Neeta could just imagine how Mark had dealt with that. He'd probably borne the talk and glances like he had when James Eicher came into the store—with barely held stoicism. But underneath that? Now she knew, he had been hurting. What a horrible experience that must have been for him. He took himself out to supper after a long day of work, only to be treated like a pariah the whole time!

After praying last night and speaking to her mother now, Waneta was even more determined to show Mark a different side of herself. She might still be a little wary of him, but she certainly didn't fear him. She'd never worried yesterday that he would harm her.

"I don't think the policemen got it wrong," she said slowly. "I think he was in the wrong place at the wrong time, or maybe someone just wanted him to be guilty because of his family. Or, who knows? All I do know is that his past

33

isn't any of our business. He grew up here, same as everyone else. We all need to give him the benefit of the doubt."

Her mother's happy smile faltered. "I must say I'm surprised. You sound awfully sure about this Mark Fisher, considering he's practically a stranger to ya."

"He's not a stranger. As a matter—"

Her mother interrupted. "Well, maybe I am being rather harsh." Frowning, she continued. "He was a sweet little boy, now that I think about it. Always trying so hard to care for his little brother."

"I had forgotten about that."

"Me, too," Mamm said as she stood up and poured herself a bowlful of cereal and milk.

Unlike Waneta and her father, her mother had always had a secret fondness for unhealthy breakfast options. She loved all kinds of children's cereal, Apple Jacks being her absolute favorite. A close second were chocolate Pop-Tarts, though she tried hard never to buy them.

Pop-Tarts were a sure way to make her happy, though. Neeta remembered her father bringing them home from Walmart whenever Mamm was in a particularly bad mood. They always brightened her spirits.

So did, she realized, Apple Jacks.

Now was her chance to tell her mother about her new work relationship with Mark.

34

Waiting until her mother had a mouthful of sugary cereal, she said, "Mamm, I've got something to tell ya. I'm working with Mark now."

Mamm set her spoon down and swallowed hard. "Say again?"

"Mr. Lehmann hired Mark." When the line between her mother's brows didn't ease, Waneta said simply, "His first day of work was yesterday."

"How do you feel about that?"

"To be honest, I was a little wary of him yesterday. But I feel better about him today. He seems nice enough." Okay, that was kind of a stretch, but there was a good chance that he could be nice, if she was nice, too.

"What did your father say when you told him?"

"I didn't tell him yet."

"Why not?" A bit of nervousness entered her tone. "He might have a weak heart, but he would want to know who you are around all day long. He worries about you, you know."

"I know." Her father worried about her waiting on strangers at the greenhouse, and used to ask her all kinds of questions about who she'd talked to while at work. He would have wanted to talk about Mark, too. Probably for a good long time. She hadn't been willing to do that. "I wasn't ready to talk about Mark yet," she said honestly.

"Was it because you are afraid of him? If

so, I want you to quit right now. You can always find another job."

"I'm not afraid, and I don't want to work anywhere else," she said quickly, though just yesterday she'd thought about getting a new job more than once.

Now Waneta's reticence seemed so silly. After nibbling the last of her whole wheat toast, she stood up and washed her plate in the sink. "Speaking of work, I need to get on my way. *Danke* for breakfast. I appreciate it."

"You're welcome." Standing up, her mother picked up her bowl and brought it to the sink. "Don't forget your lunch."

Dutifully, Waneta went to the refrigerator and collected her small cooler. "*Danke*, Mamm. You are sweet to always pack my lunch."

"You know I don't mind helping you."

"I know. That's why you're such a good mother, and I hope to be just like you one day."

"Ack, Neeta. The things you say."

Glad to see some color back in her mother's face, she pressed a kiss to her cheek. "Now, don't worry about me. And please, don't worry Daed about my job. I'll talk to him when the time is right."

"Your father can handle anything if he needs to handle it. The Lord will help. Now, let's talk about this Mark some more."

"Sorry. I can't."

Her mother followed her to the back door. "Neeta, please be careful around this boy. He might not be everything you think he is."

"He's not a boy, Mamm. And he might not be everything you think he is, either."

"Well, this man, he might be up to no good. He might be biding his time or something." She snapped her fingers. "Then, poof! You are hurt."

"Or he might be simply trying to fit in and settle down. Now, I really must go. See you tonight." She smiled as she grabbed her tote bag and purse and hurried out the door.

It was a blessing that her mother didn't follow her.

After placing everything in the basket on her bicycle, she pushed off and headed to work. As she rode down the windy road, feeling heat already coming off the pavement, Waneta prayed that she wasn't being more optimistic about Mark than was wise.

And while she didn't think Mark was going to hurt her, she certainly was a long way from feeling comfortable around him.

She didn't know if she ever would be.

Chapter 5

August 5

Waneta Cain was difficult to understand.

All day yesterday, she'd appeared to go out of her way to avoid him. She'd barely met his eyes; she certainly hadn't spoken to him unless she had to. As much as it had hurt, it was nothing more than he'd expected.

But today? Well, she was acting different.

Really different.

From the moment she greeted him in her robin's egg blue dress, she was a bright little ray of sunshine. She told him good morning. She not only didn't seem as tense around him, she even joked with him a bit.

He caught her studying him more than once, too, as if she wanted to know more about him. Not like she had yesterday. Definitely not like everyone at Bill's who stared at him last night.

No, today it seemed as if she had something new on her mind. He wondered what it was, and if she was planning to share.

He counted it as a personal blessing that the store was especially busy. He had too much to do to dwell on her abrupt change in personality.

Henry had told Mark when he'd arrived that morning to get ready to do a lot of running around, and he hadn't been mistaken. It was Friday, the beginning of the weekend. Lots of tourists came to Hart County on the weekends and stopped by the nursery on their way to tour caves or visit on the horse farms in the area.

Locals from Horse Cave and Munfordville stopped in, too. Blooms and Berries was not only known for its plants, shrubs, and gardening supplies but also for the large variety of local produce that they sold.

All three of them had been at customers' beck and call since they'd opened the door at eight. Because of that, Mark had only been treated to rude gasps and stares from a couple of people. Most just treated him with cool politeness. Being able to just do his job instead of feeling like he was an animal on display at the zoo was a relief.

The only bright spot had been when Preacher Eli had stopped by. Though Mark didn't feel as close to him as he did Henry, Eli had been instrumental in helping Mark reclaim his faith. He had an ease about him that Mark appreciated.

"Looks like you're settling in," Eli said when he brought a pair of gerbera daisies to the counter.

"I'm doing my best," Mark replied while Waneta rang Eli up.

"That's all one can ask for. Ain't so?"

"Mark is doing just fine," Waneta said with a smile. "I'm glad he's here."

Mark was surprised to hear her say that. After glancing at her curiously, he held up the two plants. "Want some help carrying these out?"

Eli laughed. "I ain't that much older than you. If I canna handle two daisies, I've got a big problem."

Mark, Waneta, and the next people in line chuckled as he left. Once again, the preacher had brought light into a room with only a few words.

That light had stayed with Mark for the next hour . . . until Henry had appeared. "If any two people deserve a lunch break, it is you both," he said as he walked in the front door after chatting with a pair of farmers in the parking lot. "It's sure been busy."

"It has," Neeta said. "I'm glad. It always makes the day go faster."

"Indeed." Turning to Mark, Henry said, "You've been a big help today. It was nice to be able to count on you for all that heavy lifting."

Mark dismissed the praise. He hated being thanked for doing something that should have been a given for all of them. "You shouldn't be lifting anything at all," said Mark. "Especially not anything over twenty pounds. And neither should you," he added, looking at Neeta. "I don't know how you two have managed so well without me all this time."

"I wouldn't say we managed well," Waneta said. "You definitely have an easier time carrying around bags of mulch than I do."

"I should. Those bags are at least thirty pounds!" Mark exclaimed.

Henry laughed. "I'm old but not that old. And Neeta is stronger than she looks. But don't forget that we have Ben Hilty coming in on Saturdays now. He's young and strong. We've put him to work from time to time as well."

"I don't know who he is."

"He lives over in Munfordville. Just turned fourteen. But he's eager to be of assistance."

Mark barely stopped himself from commenting on Ben's age. Fourteen was young, but not too young to share some burdens. After all, he'd been practically managing his whole house by the time he was thirteen.

Henry didn't seem to be perturbed by Mark's silence at all. Brushing his hands together, he said, "Let's stop worrying so much. Today has been *gut*."

"Indeed it has," Waneta said with a smile.

"I think it's time for you two to take your lunch break," Henry said as he took his place back behind the counter.

"Both of us?" Mark asked. Hadn't he just pointed out that Henry needed his help?

Waneta looked agitated. "Henry, we don't have to eat together. That doesn't seem fair to you."

41

"Nonsense. I'll be fine. I was managing this nursery for quite a while before you came along, girl." Making a shooing motion with his hands, he said, "Go on, now. Sit down and rest. Both of you. I'll see you in forty-five minutes."

Mark hesitated. "That seems too long for lunch. How about—"

"If I need help, I'll call ya," Henry said, his voice firm. "Now, go on. I'm tired of bickering."

Mark wasn't sure where to eat. Yesterday, he'd eaten his lunch in the storage room. But he'd been alone. Now, the thought of sharing that small space with Waneta seemed like it might be awkward, especially since she hadn't seemed all that thrilled about eating with him.

But if he didn't eat in the storage room, he didn't know where else to be.

"Come on, Mark," Waneta said as she walked toward the back door. "Mr. Lehmann is right. We deserve a break. But let's not eat in the storage room. It's so dark and cramped in there."

"Where do you suggest?"

"How about we go get our lunches and sit outside?"

Now his coworker was not only being friendly, she was trying to get them to spend time together. She wasn't being shy about it, neither. Feeling at a loss for words, Mark followed her. What was she up to now?

Waneta's body was betraying her. Her heart

was racing, her face felt flushed, and a fine sheen of perspiration was coating her brow. Though she was doing her best to pretend that she was no longer afraid of Mark, it seemed her body hadn't caught on to that idea. She hoped he didn't notice these sudden changes. If he did, it would be awfully embarrassing.

"Waneta?"

"*Jah?*"

"Care to share why you are looking like you are trying your best not to throw up?"

"I'm not about to throw up. And even if I was, I wouldn't want to share that information."

As they continued to walk toward the old picnic table in the back of the property, Mark kept darting concerned looks her way. "Is it me? Is the thought of being alone with me scaring you that much?"

"*Nee.*"

Since it was too late to back out from eating lunch with him, she hoped for both of their sakes that he just thought the hot summer day was getting the best of her.

As they sat down, he opened his mouth like he was about to ask something, but then closed it.

Yet again she was somehow making things worse between them instead of better. After putting her cooler on the worn metal picnic table, she silently blessed her meal and dug in.

Mark was moving far more slowly as he

grabbed his own lunch, which looked like it was in an old Walmart bag. After he took a large bite out of his peanut butter sandwich, she felt pretty embarrassed. She easily had three times the amount of food that he did. Why had her mother packed so much anyway? No one needed that much food!

"I haven't eaten a peanut butter sandwich in years," she said. "Is it good?"

He shrugged. "Good enough. It was easy to make. That's all that counted early this morning." He took another bite.

"I know what that is like. I'm always running late in the morning." She swallowed as she opened her own container of leftover chicken and rice. Also in her cooler were four oatmeal cookies, two apples, and some macaroni salad.

As he peered into her cooler, his lips twitched. "You are such a tiny thing. I never thought you'd be such a big eater."

"I'm not." Though, of course, her sizable lunch said otherwise.

"Ah."

"I usually share my cookies with Mr. Lehmann." So, that explained two of the cookies. "And, well, I guess I'm always a little afraid of going hungry. This job is tough on an empty stomach."

"True enough."

Mark was just about done with his sandwich. She,

on the other hand, had enough for several more people. It was a lot—even for her. She realized then that Mamm had been trying to feed Mark, too.

Pulling out the container of macaroni salad, she said, "Obviously I brought too much. Would you like this? And maybe an apple?"

He looked at it suspiciously. "Why?"

"Because I brought too much food and I thought you might still be hungry." Nudging the salad his way, she said, "Please, help yourself. You'd be doing me a favor."

He shook his head impatiently. "I meant talking to me. You said good morning and kind of smiled at me. Now here you are, eating lunch with me and offering me your food. Why?"

She wasn't really sure if it had more to do with concern for him or worry about how she felt about herself. She hoped she wasn't that self-serving, but at the moment she wasn't sure. Maybe she'd never been tested?

To buy herself time, she attempted to tease. "I didn't kind of smile. I did smile, Mark."

"Whatever. You know what I mean." Before she could answer, he blurted, "Is it because of your mother?"

"What does she have to do with me offering you an apple?"

"I saw her at Bill's last night. She kept eyeing me like I was going to either take her purse or yank her into a dark corner."

Because she could actually imagine her mother looking like that, she laughed nervously. "Surely, you exaggerate."

"Yeah. Probably. But I'm still asking you."

He had a right to be answered, too. "Maybe I just felt bad about yesterday," she said at last. "Maybe I realized that I should have been more welcoming to you."

But instead of dropping the subject, he shifted, looking even more intimidating. "Only *maybe?*"

She was starting to hate how he wasn't letting her off easy. "Look, I'm not proud of the way I behaved yesterday. I was, well, nervous around you."

"Because of what you thought I did."

She nodded. "*Jah.* But also because you weren't friendly. You seemed angry and tense as well. But even though you acted that way, I know I should have been more welcoming. I hardly spoke to you at all and it was your very first day. I am sorry."

Immediately, his whole posture changed. He tensed up and his judgmental expression was replaced by a look of concern. "Are you still nervous?"

"*Nee.*" When he continued to simply watch her warily, she amended her words. "Actually, yes. I think I might still be a little nervous, but I'm trying not to be. I'll get better."

"I would never hurt you."

This conversation was most definitely not going in the direction she'd intended. Why couldn't they have simply eaten in peace? Meeting his gaze, she saw that his dark eyes seemed almost liquid. He was being sincere.

He was truly concerned that she could be afraid of him.

"I know you wouldn't hurt me," she whispered.

"Do you? Do you really?"

"I know I need to learn to trust you."

"I didn't hurt Bethany. The sheriff didn't just find me innocent, I *was* innocent, Waneta."

She figured that was a pretty important point. As she did the night before, she imagined what life must have been like for him. He'd been accused of a terrible crime and had been asked to prove his innocence. Wasn't he supposed to have been presumed innocent until proven otherwise?

Done with the leftovers, she closed the container and placed one of the apples on her napkin. "I don't actually know you, Mark. I know who you are, and I remember you and your brother in school." She paused, then decided to lay everything out. "Even back when we were all little, I heard stories about your parents, too. I know they left the order. I heard they made a lot of mistakes. I also know that you are living in your old house. I can only imagine how hard that must be."

She paused again when she noticed that he

seemed stunned by her words. "Even though I know all that, I realize we have much to learn about each other. Just like I don't know you very well, you don't know me."

He blinked. "That is true."

Now that they were finally making amends, she smiled slightly. "Mark, please believe me. I don't fear you. At all."

"I never thought you'd bring all of that up. You surprised me."

"I never intended to bring it up," she said. "I thought it would be rude. But just now, it felt like it would be rude not to bring it up. Since I like this job and we're going to be working together, I was hoping we could simply learn to get along. Can you forgive me enough to do that?"

"There's nothing for me to forgive," replied Mark. "And you are right. We don't know each other. I'd like to fix that, though."

She smiled in relief. "I'd like that, too."

Though he didn't exactly smile, he seemed to relax. Reaching out, he said, "Hey. Are you done with your fork?"

She looked at him in confusion. After all she'd just said, that is what he asks her? "I am."

"*Gut.*" He picked it up, opened the Tupperware container, speared two macaroni noodles, and popped them in his mouth.

She swallowed, felt her cheeks flush. "I could have washed that for you."

"It looked fine."

"But, I . . ." She didn't want to say the obvious, but didn't he think using her fork was, well, kind of personal?

"Are you sick?"

"*Nee.*"

"Then it's fine," he said as he speared a red pepper. "This is good, Waneta."

"*Danke.*"

"Did you make it?"

"*Jah.* My mother cooks a lot, but I made the salad."

He took three bites, then closed the container and put the fork on top of it. Now he was biting into the red apple she'd given him.

She bit into hers as well, tried to concentrate on the tart, sweet taste of the Gala apple on her tongue. But for some reason, she could only focus on how happy he looked eating his.

"I'd compliment you on the apple, too, but I think God had more to do with making it than you did."

She giggled. "You would be right. I love apples."

"What else do you love?"

Glad that the tension between them had broken, she leaned back and smiled. "Hmm. Well, I love walking in the woods, for one. Gardening, too. And snow, even though most people don't care for it much. Oh! And walking in Horse Cave.

I love exploring the cave system. I think it's fascinating."

"You really like the outdoors, don't you?"

"I love it. Though my *mamm* taught me to cook and clean and sew, of course, I don't love those things all that much." Smiling at him, she said, "What about you?"

"What do I love?"

"Come on. If I'm sharing, you are, too."

"Okay, then. I love clean, fresh cotton sheets on my bed. I love silence in the house. I like dogs. I like hot, sunny days." With a wink, he added, "And macaroni salad."

"It seems we're at odds with each other, since I like the winter and you like the summer."

"We like different things, but I don't know if one would say we're at odds with each other. I hope not." After he threw his sack and apple core in the trash, he turned to her. "Thank you again," he said almost formally. "This was nice."

She realized he was going to go back into the store. "You're going back already? I think we still have fifteen minutes."

"It's early, but I don't mind. I don't want Henry to have to work by himself any longer. See you in fifteen minutes."

Alone again, she thought about her little speech, and how off guard he'd looked when she'd mentioned his parents.

She thought about his list of loves. Realized

50

that they were all things she took for granted, things he'd most likely missed when he was a boy growing up in that house.

Then she thought about him using her fork and eating the food she'd brought.

And she wondered why she was so pleased that things had turned out the way they had.

Chapter 6

August 5

*Y*ou are so foolish, Mark chided himself as he walked home Friday evening after work.

Remembering their lunch together, he grimaced. He'd finally had the opportunity to show how much he'd grown. But instead of simply eating lunch and talking about easy things, he'd delved into something far more personal.

Really personal.

What had possessed him to ask her about things she loved?

It had been obvious that he'd taken her off guard.

Then he'd gone and used her fork. He'd known doing something so personal and unexpected would make her uncomfortable. But he'd done it anyway.

Who in the world even did things like that? One would think he'd actually been in prison for the last two years, the way he was behaving. His parents might have done a lot of things wrong, but they had taught him the basics of getting along with others. He did know the correct way to behave.

If he didn't learn to apply some self-control around Waneta Cain, he was going to do or say something to make her wary enough to complain to Henry about him.

He wouldn't blame her if she did that, either. She had every right to complain if the new employee was making her uncomfortable. Then Henry would have to make a decision about whether to keep him on or not. And if it came down to choosing him or her?

Well, he knew who Henry would ask to stay.

Mark would be out of a job so fast, he wouldn't know what hit him.

He needed this job, too. He wanted to live in Horse Cave and fix up his old house. He wanted to show everyone in the area that he really was better than they believed him to be. He wanted to show himself that very same thing. He should be doing everything he possibly could to keep this job and make Henry glad he took a chance hiring him. He should be working hard and keeping his head down. Not acting too forward and familiar with Waneta Cain.

As he continued walking home, taking time to notice that several people were on their front porches and watching him walk by, he analyzed their lunch some more.

And realized that Waneta had actually stopped

being nervous for a little bit. She'd even smiled at him, too. It hadn't looked strained, either. Instead, it had seemed genuine.

It had made him feel good inside. Almost too good, because it had even made him imagine that he could have a chance with her one day.

For a while there, they'd talked, and their conversation hadn't been stilted or full of long, awkward silences. Instead, it had been easy. Almost relaxed.

He'd felt something happening between them and it felt an awful lot like acceptance. Acceptance was something he hadn't felt in years.

It also wasn't something that he'd experienced in a long time. Maybe that meant that they could eventually be friends. Maybe even more than friends.

"Mark Fisher, is that you?"

Stopping, he turned to see Lora Weaver walking right behind him. "Lora?"

She nodded and smiled, increasing her pace.

Mark didn't even try to hide his surprise. Lora had been his female counterpart in Horse Cave when they were growing up. Both of them had sad home lives that they tried desperately to keep hidden. Her father had taken off when she was just a toddler, ignoring both his marriage vows and promises to the church. His actions had left Lora's mom alone with four children, no income, and a fierce depression.

Lora used to shyly admit that on some days their mother never got out of bed. As the years passed, Lora took on more responsibility for her younger siblings and became bitter and angry during the week, and more than a little wild during the weekends.

She'd always said she was going to leave Hart County the first day she could, and never look back. She'd done that, too. She left when she was sixteen or thereabouts.

"I sure never thought I'd see you again," she said when she reached his side.

"I was just thinking the same thing about you. I canna believe you are here."

"I know." Looking sheepish, she continued. "I swore I'd never come back if it was the last place on earth. But, here I am."

"You moved back?" He didn't even try to hide his astonishment.

She lifted one shoulder. "I did. Fourteen months ago." Her voice drifted off. "I suppose everyone does things at one time or another that they never intended."

Though he agreed, he thought she was generalizing her return a little too lightly. Lora had been vocal about her disdain for their hometown.

But he didn't have any desire to hurt her feelings. "It's all part of life, I guess," he murmured. "Maybe."

"*Jah*. Maybe." When she smiled in a condescending way, he studied her. She was wearing dark-washed jeans and a snug-fitting black tank top. Bright-blue bra straps directed his eye to her shoulders. Worn rubber flip-flops were on her feet. Her toenails were painted dark purple and she had a couple of silver earrings in each ear. She looked good. Free-spirited.

Pretty much like any other English girl about her age.

And the complete opposite of Waneta. "Why did you come back? What happened?" he asked.

"That's the same question I was going to ask you."

"Henry told me that he'd heard that I inherited my parents' old house and decided to come back and live there."

She raised her eyebrows. "Really? I would have thought you would have wanted to stay as far away from there as possible."

"It's paid for." He also wasn't willing to give up on his life here. Though his home life had been so bad, there was still a stubborn part of him that kept hoping to make things better. It was how he'd survived his childhood.

Hearing from Henry had felt like a sign, too. He'd secretly felt like the Lord was telling him that it was time to return to his past and make things better.

Maybe even transform it?

When he returned, he'd met with Preacher Eli and gotten baptized. Then he decided to transform the house, just like he'd been seeking to transform himself.

Then there was Henry. Henry needed him and Mark craved the man's love like a child craved a mother's arms.

Lora nodded. "Makes sense. Paid for is good."

"What about you?" he asked again, since she still hadn't answered his question. "Why did you come back? I thought you were long gone."

"I was." Her lips thinned. "It's a long story, but I guess it's enough to say that I discovered that the big world ain't all that easy." She paused. "But things have been good here. I'm working over at Bill's Diner."

"I was there last night. I didn't see you, though."

"I had the night off. You'll have to come back soon. I'll introduce you to the other waitresses there. Everyone's real nice."

"I'm glad you are happy at your job. Hey, where are you living? In your old place, too?"

"I am, if you can believe that. My youngest sister, Beth, is pretty much my mother's favorite. She married an Amish man and lives on a forty-acre farm. Mamm lives with her and helps mind their six *kinner*. My other sister Amanda lived in the house until she and her husband could afford a bigger place. So she gave it to me. I'm the charity case."

"What about your other sister? I forget her name."

Lora's expression shuttered. "Martha died."

"I'm sorry to hear that."

She lifted her shoulder again. "Her death is a long story."

"She get cancer or something?"

"*Nee.*" Sounding strained, she said, "In a nutshell, Martha managed to get into even more trouble than me. We all thought something bad would happen to her one day. We were right."

Martha's story reminded him of Calvin. And that, of course, put him on edge. He was trying to move forward. To make something of himself. To create a new reputation. Not rehash and relive all the bad ones.

Shoving his hands into his pockets, he awkwardly stepped back. "Well, ah, good to see you. I've been working all day and I'm a sweaty mess. I'd best be getting on home."

"I understand. Do you mind if we walk a little further together? I pass your street on the way to my place."

Her offer made perfect sense and Lora had been nothing but pleasant—unlike the majority of the people at Bill's last night. So he didn't understand why he suddenly felt uncomfortable. "Yeah, sure."

Looking pleased, she started walking. As he stayed by her side, she began pointing out different people's houses. He listened and looked with only the smallest bit of interest. He didn't remember most of the people she named. He wasn't sure what to do with the information she was handing him, either.

"That place now belongs to the Swartz family," she said. "Remember Daniel?"

"*Jah.* You had a crush on him something awful."

"Oh, that. That didn't mean anything."

"You sure? 'Cause I kind of remember you mooning over him one Sunday evening at a singing."

"I didn't." She laughed. "All right, you caught me. I mean I didn't moon over him too much."

He grinned, finally feeling more relaxed. "I'm glad you called out to me, Lora. This is the most relaxed I've felt in a week."

"Really? Now that's a shame. You always were so nice." Her gaze landed on him fondly before drifting to the street. "Unlike some people."

Wondering who she was referring to, he gazed at the street.

And saw Waneta riding her bicycle, her tote bag and little cooler in the basket behind her seat.

He froze, just as she glanced his way. Their eyes met for a long moment before she looked nervously at Lora, then turned her head as she rode on.

Seeing him with Lora had obviously made Waneta uncomfortable. He wondered if it was Lora herself or the fact that he was out walking with her.

"It must be pretty hard to go through life as perfect and holier-than-thou as Waneta Cain," Lora muttered.

Mark frowned. She'd stretched out Waneta's name so it had sounded awkward and almost like a whine.

"That ain't fair. She's a nice woman."

"Oh, she's nice, all right. Nice to the right people. Not nice to people like you and me."

"I work with her," he said. "She's been nothing but kind to me."

Hurt flashed in her eyes. "Really? Well, if she is, then that is surely an accomplishment. Waneta don't give too many people the time of day. Especially people she thinks are beneath her."

Mark hated that Lora was speaking so disparagingly about her. "You're being awfully harsh. Waneta hasn't been like that to me. Henry Lehmann thinks the world of her."

"Huh. Well, she's looked right through me more than once. If she's treating you different, it must be because she feels sorry for ya or something."

He didn't like anything Lora was saying. Not

60

the insinuation that Waneta wasn't kind. Not how she was implying that she wasn't as good a person as Waneta. "My house is down the street," he said abruptly. "See you, Lora."

Looking puzzled, she stopped and stared at him. "That's it?"

"*Jah*. I told you I was going home."

"Oh." As if she was summoning a smile, she said brightly, "Hey, you know what? It's Friday night. What are you doing for the rest of it? Want some company?"

He wasn't sure what she wanted from him, but he wasn't ready to give it. He knew he wasn't in the right mindset to tackle Lora's animosity toward Waneta. "*Nee*. I just want to relax. See you later, Lora."

Hurt filled her gaze. "Oh. Well, um, yeah . . . sure. Bye, Mark."

As he turned down his street, he glanced up at the sky. *What had that been about, God? Did you need me to remember my past and how far apart I was from Waneta?*

Passing house after house, most looking bigger and more cleaned up and taken care of than he remembered, he thought of something else. Maybe the Lord was telling him the exact opposite. Maybe He had brought Lora into Mark's life to show just how far he'd come from his childhood, both physically and emotionally.

No longer did he have to be judged by his past,

or by factors that had always been out of his control. Instead, he could present himself to be the man he'd always hoped he could get to be. He could show people like Waneta just how much he had changed.

Now, that was a good thought. A promising thought. Something to give praise for.

Feeling almost happy, Mark walked up his steps, pulled out his house key, and grabbed the mail from the box on the edge of the porch. This was normal. He had nothing to fear but his memories. Everything was going to be all right.

And as for Lora? Well, he'd just have to do a little bit of praying and thinking about that. Maybe she'd been reaching out to him because she only needed a friend.

Or maybe she needed some guidance and he was the best person to offer it to her. If that was the case, he would do his best to be the person she needed him to be.

When he walked in, he released a ragged sigh. At least he was home alone now. For the rest of the evening, he was going to do his best to forget about everything but eating a big supper and relaxing on the back porch. It had been a hard, hot week.

But just as he was about to sit down and sift through the mail, he noticed that some cushions from his couch were displaced. The book he'd left on the side table had been flipped over.

Hurrying to the kitchen, he saw that one of the four chairs around the table had been moved. The paper and yesterday's mail was scattered on the counter as well.

Someone had been in his house while he'd been working and they hadn't been shy about letting him know that.

Who could it have been?

Chapter 7

Friday, August 5

Stuffing her fingertips into the front pockets of her jeans, Lora watched Mark as he walked away from her. She tried not to let his refusal to spend more time together get her down. But it still did.

She wondered what had set him off. At first he'd seemed genuinely happy to see her. Then, in an abrupt turnaround, he acted as if he was embarrassed that he even knew her name. What had she done wrong? Had she pushed too hard to connect with him again? Though the girls at work didn't seem to mind when she asked them questions or shared personal information, it might have been too forward for a private man like Mark.

Or maybe it was that they'd both changed too much. Mark was even more subdued than he had been as a boy. Then, of course, she was now obviously no longer Amish.

That seemed like a better guess. Mark Fisher always had been so straight and upstanding. He liked to follow the rules and liked it when other people did that, too. She'd always thought Mark cared more than most about how things looked. He never had liked it when things were out of order.

Not even when he was just nine or ten years old.

No matter what his parents did and no matter how much he looked like he'd needed a few solid meals and a fresh change of clothes, Mark had always acted as if he'd come from the best, most proper family in the county. Well, he'd tried to pretend that, though everyone knew his home life wasn't any better than hers.

Maybe he was afraid renewing their friendship would taint him somehow. That being seen with her would ruin his reputation, such that it was. Lora hoped that wasn't the case, but she could see that happening.

Calvin used to joke about his big brother, saying Mark was rebelling by being everything good since their parents were so bad. Lora would roll her eyes at statements like that, but she'd secretly admired Mark for wanting to be someone better than the people who'd raised him.

She'd thought it was admirable, but not necessarily possible. 'Course, she'd also done her share of pretending when she was a child. She'd told herself that living in a broken-down house with a broken-down mother wasn't so bad. She'd even got real good at pretending not to notice the looks of disdain half the population of Horse Cave shot her way when she and her sisters would wander around town late at night, doing anything to avoid going home. Sometimes she found she could even ignore other kids' cruel taunts about her ill-fitting clothes and missing father.

But as far as forgetting . . . well, that had been another story. She still woke up once or twice a month in a panic, cruel words and taunts ringing in her head from people like Bethany Williams.

Even now, thinking about Bethany made Lora cringe. She'd had the face of an angel, and the ability to convince every adult in the county that her soul was just as pure. Lora knew from experience that it wasn't. Lora had been skilled at delivering snide comments under her breath. Her victims would be hurt, but would be too afraid of her retaliation to ever speak up.

Though she'd kept her opinions to herself, Lora had been sure that Mark hadn't been the man who'd assaulted her. Bethany had been too willful and erratic for Mark. He had avoided her at all costs.

Shaking her head, she shoved all thoughts of Bethany away. That was in the past and she was doing her best to focus on the present. She needed to continue to count her blessings. She was back in Horse Cave and she was doing okay.

When her sister Amanda had called to offer her

the house, Lora hadn't even acted like she wasn't grateful. Losing Martha to a drug overdose had been horrible. Discovering that she'd been living in a dirty room in downtown Cincinnati the last months of her life had been a blow to all of them.

Now she and her two remaining sisters were trying their best to forge a new relationship together. She didn't have much in common with them, but they'd all learned how difficult it was to dwell only on each other's differences.

Even their mother was trying to make amends for the damage she'd done to all of them.

While Lora doubted she'd ever be able to completely forgive her, Lora was able to at least share a meal with her every once in a while.

When her house was in sight, Lora let her thoughts drift back to Mark. Reflecting on their conversation, she realized that Mark's demeanor had changed the moment Waneta Cain rode by. It was obvious now that he was anxious to put some distance between them.

What was it about Waneta that he admired so much? When Lora shared her feelings about the woman, Mark jumped to Waneta's defense like a Doberman.

Actually, he'd defended Waneta like someone who was a very close friend, mentioning all of her qualities again and again. It didn't seem like he agreed with anything Lora was saying about Waneta. It was as if he didn't remember anything about their past; didn't remember how the two of them used to walk home together with twin feelings of dread while girls like Waneta barely looked their way.

Could Mark really have forgotten the way Waneta and her friends would giggle at Lora and her sisters—when they weren't ignoring them? How Waneta had gotten new dresses and backpacks and school supplies all the time? How she'd brought enormous lunches in her pail every day? How she'd share only with her friends while he and Lora went hungry?

Surely, he hadn't forgotten that!

But it hadn't seemed to matter. It was almost like he was sweet on Waneta. Maybe he was, she realized with a sinking feeling. Maybe Mark had decided to set his sights up high and he didn't want to associate with people like Lora when he could align himself with innocent girls like Waneta.

Lora trudged up her front porch steps and took a seat in one of the three white wicker chairs that Amanda had bought when she lived there.

Only when she sat down did she notice poor Katie Eicher gardening in her front flower beds. She was on her hands and knees, painstakingly pulling weeds in her vegetable garden. She looked hot, sweaty, and tired.

Like she usually did, except when she went to church.

James, her husband, was a bully. There really was no other name for it. Lora heard him yell at Katie often. He wasn't shy about it. He certainly never attempted to keep their private life private. For what seemed—to Lora at least—increasingly dumb reasons, James would deride his wife, put her down.

It was hard to hear and even more difficult to watch.

Looking over at her, Lora sensed that Katie was trying her best to get the gardening done before her husband came home. Remembering the pot of sun tea she'd made two days before, Lora went inside and filled two Mason jars with ice, the strong tea, and two generous spoonfuls of sugar. Then, before she thought better of it, she walked across the street.

Taking care to keep her voice relaxed and friendly, she smiled wide. "Hiya, Katie, I brought you a glass of tea."

When Katie looked up, Lora almost gasped. One of Katie's eyes was swollen shut. The skin surrounding it was black and blue. "Oh, Katie. That has to hurt," she said.

Gingerly, Katie pressed one hand to her face. "It ain't so bad," she said in a rush. "Is it?"

Not knowing what to say that wouldn't make Katie feel worse, Lora settled for holding out one of the jars. "Would you like some?"

"*Danke*. It's warm out here. I was getting

69

thirsty." She took a long sip, then another one. "It's *gut* tea, Lora. You always do such a good job with that."

"It's only sun tea."

"Mine never tastes as good." Katie smiled, then seemed to recall herself. "I had better finish up my chores. James will be home soon."

It was pretty obvious that her neighbor was worried about getting everything done before her husband returned. "Do you need some help?" she asked. She didn't mind. The work would also serve to help keep her mind off her conversation with Mark.

"Doing what?"

"Weeding?" Katie looked so surprised, Lora chuckled. "Just because I'm not dressed Amish and don't keep a garden don't mean that I've never tended one. I can pull weeds as well as anyone."

"Oh. Of course." Biting her bottom lip, Katie gazed at her garden. "Well, now . . . thank you, but I'll be all right."

"Do you not want my help? Or is something else bothering you?"

Katie pressed her hand to her face again. "I shouldn't really talk about it."

There was her opening. She needed to say something about her face. She needed to know that even though they weren't especially close, Lora cared and wanted to help. Kneeling down, she looked directly at her. "Katie, when did that happen? Last night or this morning?"

Keeping her eyes averted, she nervously pressed a hand to her cheek again. "This morning." Lowering her hand, she looked at Lora directly. "I guess it really does look bad. Ain't so?"

"I'm more concerned about how you are faring instead of how you look." When Katie seemed confused, Lora said, "Your cheek is really swollen and your eye looks worse than blood-shot. Can you see out of it?"

"Kind of."

"You know, something could be really wrong. Do you think you need to go to the doctor? If so, I'll help you get an appointment. I'll go with you, too."

She paled. "I don't need to see the *doktah*." Raising a hand, her next words tumbled out in a rush. "Please, don't worry. I'll be okay. Hopefully my face will look much better by Sunday."

Lora knew now that if Katie's swelling hadn't gone down or if her eye wasn't completely back to normal by church, then Katie would simply stay home. "I want to help you. Will you let me?"

"Help? With what?"

"With everything. Do you feel safe at home?"

Abruptly, Katie set the Mason jar on the ground. "I don't know what you mean."

Lora wasn't in the mood to go through the

motions and pretend that Katie hurt her eye by walking into a wall or some other sort of nonsense.

But she also didn't know her well enough to be completely direct with her and say that she knew James hurt her. So she simply shrugged. "I think you do know what I mean, but if you don't want to talk about it, I understand."

Looking frazzled, Katie thrust the jar into her hands. "Here. Thank you for bringing it to me, but now I must get back to work."

"Just because you don't want to talk about your eye doesn't mean you can't drink my tea. Does it?" Attempting to smile, she said, "How about I help you weed for a while?" Scanning the garden, she said, "I'll take the row of squash."

"You had better not," she said in a rush. "James would get upset."

"Why? He doesn't want you to have help?"

"He wouldn't want me to have you in our yard."

Not even to weed? "Why is that?" she asked slowly. "Is it because I'm not Amish?"

If anything, Katie looked even more worried. "That is one of the reasons." After darting a glance down their empty street, she stepped toward her door. "Now, I'm sorry, but I really must go. Good-bye."

When she turned her back again, Lora felt as if she'd been rejected for the second time in less than an hour. It seemed that no matter what happened, she wasn't good enough company. Not even good enough company to pull weeds.

Feeling more tired than ever, she got back on her feet and carried the two jars back to her house.

After she looked inside, she looked around. It was still silent, too big, and empty. She had returned even though she'd promised herself never to return. And suddenly, it was too much. The quiet. The memories. The time. She needed a way not to think of it for a while.

Thinking a six-pack of beer and maybe a bottle of tequila would take the edge off, she stuffed a couple of bills in her back pocket and left again.

She didn't bother turning the lock. No one would come to her house unless they had no other options.

She was living proof of that.

Chapter 8

Sunday, August 7

W hat did you think about Preacher Eli's sermon?" June Gingerich asked Waneta as they helped to clean the four long tables that had been set up to serve the church luncheon. "It was pretty forceful, don'tcha think? Preacher Eli doesn't usually sound so stern."

Waneta nodded as she considered her friend's statement. In her usual way, June had focused on the heart of the matter. "I thought he was going to start calling out names, he was so upset about how some folks were acting. It caught me off guard. I've hardly ever seen him without a smile on his face. Who knew he could be so solemn?"

"He's been solemn with me when I've gotten counseling," June said. "But he never seemed like he was actually mad at me." Lowering her voice, she added, "I overheard two women say that they thought he was treating them like naughty *kinner*. They really weren't happy."

"I know his sermon probably caused quite a few people to be uncomfortable, but I think his

74

stern manner was necessary," Waneta whispered. After darting a look around to make sure no one could hear, she added, "After all, there are some people here who certainly do need a talking to. Forgiveness is something we should all take seriously. It's one of the backbones of our lives, after all."

"I hear what you're saying, but I don't think Eli was simply talking about forgiveness." After bending down to pick up a couple of stray napkins that had fallen, June lowered her voice. "I think he was actually talking about Mark Fisher. I think he was telling us that we should all try to forgive him."

After double-checking that Mark was out of earshot, Waneta nodded. "I think that's who Preacher Eli was talking about, too. Mark has returned and he wants to be part of our church community. It is wrong for some people to treat him like he has the plague."

June shook her head. "I hear what you're saying, but I think you are being a bit too generous, Neeta. What Preacher Eli said was shocking. He offended a lot of people. Why, I thought my mother was going to bite her tongue, she was trying so hard to keep her feelings to herself."

"Since all those ladies are currently gathering in a tight circle, I don't think she waited too long," Waneta said drily.

June shrugged. "Who can blame them?"

"Mark deserves forgiveness. I, for one, would hate to come back to my parents' *haus* with a cloud hanging over me. I really would hate to realize that nobody wanted me to be there, too."

"I would hate that, too. But what if they are right? What if he really is a dangerous criminal?"

Moving to the third table, Waneta shook her head. "He's not. What you are hearing is merely malicious gossip. It doesn't have any truth to it."

"But what if it does? After all, a lot of people don't want Mark here. A lot of people whose opinions I respect."

"So?"

"So? Well, so many people can't be wrong."

Waneta felt a bit like she was on a sinking ship and trying her hardest to bail out the water with a measuring cup. But still, she had to hold firm. Mark needed support. "I think differently. So does Preacher Eli."

Leaning closer, June said, "A lot of people, me included, even worry about you working with him at the nursery. I don't have a good feeling about that. I'm worried you are going to really regret it."

"Please don't. I've worked with Mark a whole week now. So far, he's been a real *gut* worker. He's also been a lot of help. Mr. Lehmann needed someone strong and able to help him."

"I thought Henry hired Mark because he felt sorry for him."

Privately, she didn't think it mattered why Henry Lehmann hired Mark. Even if he had only hired him at first because he'd felt sorry for him, Mark had more than proved his worth, even during the few days he'd been there.

"June, what matters is that everyone needs to take Preacher Eli's words to heart. What he said was important. And true." She felt so passionate, her voice rose. "We all need to stop judging others and casting stones. We also all need to seek forgiveness. I've witnessed some people be unkind to Mark at the nursery. My mother said that everyone was looking at him and gossiping at Bill's, too."

After she wiped down the last table, June braced a hand on her hip. "You sure sound high and mighty on his account."

Stung by her tone, Neeta paused. "What is that supposed to mean?"

"It means, I never figured you would be attempting to go against the rest of us for someone like Mark Fisher," she retorted, dismay heavy in her voice.

"Mark can't help where he came from."

"My parents said that more problems are going to happen around here now that he's back."

"They don't know that."

"And you don't know that they're wrong,

either." Sounding more sure of herself, she said, "Waneta, I think you should start looking for another job."

"June!"

"I'm only trying to help you," she said, then looked just beyond Neeta. "I'm only trying to make sure you are being cautious and careful."

It was more than obvious now that June hadn't taken anything from Preacher Eli's sermon to heart. "I think you are being judgmental. You are casting stones without a care about who they hurt. I think you are making a big mistake and that you are going to regret it," Waneta bit out, anger thick in her voice. "I look forward to the day you realize that, too."

"I guess you've made your choice," June said in a huff. "Now it's only a matter of time before he hurts you. When that happens and you realize how reckless you've been, come find me. We'll talk then."

Waneta stared in shock as June picked up two plastic containers filled with leftover lunchmeat and walked away.

What had just happened? One minute, June had seemed truly concerned. The next, they were going back and forth, debating Mark's character. No, it seemed they were debating their own characters, too. And their families'. How had everything gotten so bad so quickly?

"Do you want me to go talk to her?"

Startled, Neeta turned to find Mark looking directly at her, his dark eyes seeming to take in everything she was feeling. "How much did you hear?"

"Enough to know that I was the focus of your discussion. And enough to realize that she didn't agree with your perception of me."

"I'm sorry. June likes to share what's on her mind. She ain't always right, though."

"Don't apologize for her words. You can't take on how other people feel or make them change their minds if they don't want to."

"I guess not." Scanning the crowd, she searched for her best friend. She was nowhere to be seen. "I'm surprised, though. June is a really *gut* friend."

"I'm sure she is. But fear does strange things to people."

"Well, she shouldn't be afraid. There's no one in Horse Cave who is going to hurt her."

"If you're talking about me, you're right," he said lightly. "Thanks for standing up for me."

"I was standing up for you because it was the right thing to do. I'm frustrated about how much people don't seem to be able to let go of the past."

"It's understandable. The past can be a difficult thing to let go of."

Just as she was about to answer, Waneta saw

her father approach, her mother following about twenty steps behind. Bracing herself, she mumbled under her breath, "Here come my parents. Whatever they say, I want you to know I'm sorry."

Mark's eyes warmed just as her father said, "Neeta, your mother and I are about ready to leave. Are you?"

"Can you give me a couple of minutes? I was talking to Mark."

Her father smiled. "We've been talking, too."

They had? Fearing that she was just about to subject him to a whole list of invasive questions, Neeta eyed both men. "Were you discussing anything special?"

"*Nee*. We were only getting to know each other."

A flash of surprise entered Mark's eyes before he composed himself. "Don't look so worried, Neeta. Everything is fine."

Right then, her mother joined them. "Hi, Mark. We know each other, but you might not remember me. I used to help out at your school from time to time."

"I remember."

Her mother smiled. "Then you know that I'm Gettie Cain. Waneta's mother."

Before Waneta could give her mother a meaningful look, Mark said, "*Danke*. Nice to meet you as well, Gettie."

Then her *daed* shared a look with her mother and said, "Mark, do you have plans for the rest of the afternoon?"

"Not really. I had planned to work on the house. I'm trying to clean it out."

"*Jah.* I imagine that is a big job. But Sunday is for rest, not work. Why don't you come over and spend a few hours at our house? Stay for supper. We're barbecuing cheeseburgers today."

Mark was wearing an expression Neeta hadn't seen on his face before. He looked nonplussed. "W-Well . . ." he stuttered as he glanced in her direction. "I'm not sure . . ."

He was doing that for her benefit, Waneta realized. In case she didn't want him there. "I hope you accept," she interjected. "My father grills the cheeseburgers. They're very good. And my mother planted more vegetables than you can count, in pots all along the back porch and patio. The tomatoes and peppers have gone crazy! It's something to see."

"I bet," he said with a touch of humor in his voice. "Well, in that case, *danke*. I'd be happy to come over this afternoon."

Her father clapped his hands together. "*Gut.* Now, can we get along? I'm ready for a rest."

"I'll walk with you, Norman," her mother murmured. "Now that we don't have to worry about our Neeta walking alone, we can get on our way and she and Mark can follow whenever they

81

are ready. Are you sure you're going to be able to walk home? I bet we could find someone to give us a ride in their buggy."

"I've got some problems getting around, but not that many problems," Daed snapped.

Waneta had been so wrapped up in her defense of Mark, she'd forgotten just how weak her father was. Feeling that familiar knot of nerves in her stomach, she said, "We'll follow in a few minutes. Or, we can walk with you."

"No need for that. I'll be fine. You just make sure you don't tarry too long."

"I'll make sure she gets home safe," Mark said.

"I know you will. *Danke*, Mark," her father said. "Waneta has a good head on her shoulders. She ain't going to trust you for no reason."

When they were out of sight, Mark turned to her. "What just happened?"

"You have just been subjected to tornadoes Norman and Gettie. They have a way of coming in and creating havoc wherever they may be."

"That's putting it a bit strong. Ain't so?"

"You are saying that because you haven't lived with them all your life. They have a bad habit of turning everything upside down in their path."

"It's impressive. Are you upset about this? I couldn't tell. I would have tried harder to put them off if you didn't want me to visit your house."

"I want you to come over, Mark." Realizing how she sounded, she said, "I mean, I know you don't have a lot of friends here yet."

"Ah. Now I understand." He smiled, but it was strained. "Are you ready now?"

"I am." She started walking before she said anything else that could have been taken two ways. "We don't live far. Just off Second Street."

"I know where you live."

"You do?"

He coughed. "Sorry. I meant that I'm assuming you live in the same house you always have. If so, I remember it."

"I live in the same one." Laughing softly, she decided to say what was no doubt lingering on both of their minds. "We're sure doing a good job of stepping into holes, aren't we?"

"We are, but we seem to be getting a little better."

Though she felt June watching her, Waneta smiled at him.

She couldn't do anything about June's worries and doubts. Nothing except hope and pray that they were unfounded.

Chapter 9

Sunday, August 7

Mark had spent most of the previous day ripping out the linoleum that covered the first floor of his house. Someone—he wasn't sure whether it was his parents or whoever lived there before them—had covered up beautifully finished wood floors with industrial-grade linoleum.

Now that it was over twenty years old, it was yellowed and cracked. The edges next to the woodwork were peeling, too. When he'd first pulled up a corner, he imagined only finding cement underneath. Discovering a wood floor in good condition had been a nice surprise.

The hard physical labor had cleared his mind and allowed him to come to terms with the fact that someone had been in his house. But he had no idea who it could have been. He hadn't discovered that anything was damaged; nothing seemed to be missing, either. His stash of money was still exactly where he'd hidden it—taped to the bottom of his parents' old dresser.

For some reason, it seemed that the intruder had only wanted to examine everything. Mark imagined he had simply walked inside, fingered some of his items, then left.

That should have given him some measure of peace. Instead, because he couldn't figure out why anyone would want to come into his run-down house and inspect his few belongings, it had set him more on edge. He'd tossed and turned all night, half expecting to hear footsteps signaling the return of the intruder.

When he'd woken that morning to only the chaotic chirping of a pair of robins outside his window, he resolved to put those fears behind him. There was nothing he could do anyway. It wasn't like he was going to go to Sheriff Brewer and share his suspicions.

Instead, he had greeted the day with two strong cups of coffee and a short walk to the Bylers' home. They were hosting church this week.

The coffee, the almost cool morning, and the brisk walk had put Mark in a better frame of mind. By the time he arrived at the Bylers' and took his place with the other men on one side of their metal-sided barn, he felt almost at peace with himself. To his surprise, that sense of peace had stayed with him during the lengthy church service.

But as far as what was happening now?

Well, he could safely say that nothing in his life had prepared him for Norman Cain seeking him out when everyone was lining up to leave.

"Mark, stay and talk to me a while, wouldja?"

Towering over the smaller man with a far bigger reputation, Mark did the only thing he could do. He nodded.

While most everyone else passed them by, Norman sat back down. "You don't mind sitting for a spell, do you? My legs don't work like they used to."

"Of course not." He sat, too, turned slightly, and rested his elbows on his black pants.

"Let's wait a moment to talk. My ears don't work too good anymore, neither."

Nodding weakly, Mark settled in his chair and waited.

As passing seconds turned to minutes, his palms began to sweat.

Truth was, he knew all about how to sidestep conversations. He was a master at avoidance. He was extremely good at shielding his thoughts and making sure no one knew what he was thinking. All of those skills had developed because of the life he'd had at home.

He'd put them into good practice when he'd been accused of assaulting Bethany and had been taken in for questioning. The whole time Sheriff Brewer questioned him, he'd answered honestly but with no emotion. Looking back, he imagined that he'd probably sounded more interested in the weather than in Bethany's death.

No wonder Sheriff Brewer hadn't believed

Mark at first. He'd kept him in the county jail for two nights while he and his deputy had gathered evidence and questioned other people. And later, when he'd told Mark he was free to leave, Mark had taken care to keep his face an expressionless mask. Though the sheriff had obviously not trusted him, he'd let him go.

But now?

Now he couldn't remember a time when an upstanding man like Norman Cain had gone out of his way to talk to him. It had to be about Waneta. Maybe he was going to chide him for not being nicer to his daughter?

Or was it something else?

When the barn was finally empty except for the two of them, Norman breathed in deep. "Feels *gut* to have room to breathe. Some days, I think I'm going to expire in these crowded barns."

"It does get warm," Mark agreed.

"What did you think of the sermons today?"

"I enjoyed them."

Norman looked pleased. "*Gut*! Me, too."

"Ah. Is that what you wanted to talk to me about? Church today?" Maybe Norman didn't want him there?

Norman waggled his hand back and forth. "Kind of." He shifted and raised his voice. "See, it got me thinking. Well, the sermon and Waneta's lecturing did. I decided we needed to invite you over for supper."

The invitation was so unexpected, he was sure he'd misunderstood. "Excuse me?"

Norman raised his voice even louder. So loud it fairly echoed among the barn's rafters. "I want you to come over for supper this afternoon, Mark Fisher! Join me, Gettie, and Neeta."

"That's why you wanted to talk to me?"

"*Jah*. What do you say?"

"I say, Thank you."

His brow puckered. "Is that a yes?"

Mark laughed as he stood up. "*Jah*, Norman. It is a yes, all right." After all, how could he have refused an invitation like that?

"Oh! *Gut*." After he struggled to his feet, he turned to shuffle down the empty aisle. "Go find Waneta in ten minutes or so," he called out over his shoulder. "I need to go tell Gettie that you're coming over."

Watching Norman leave, Mark did something he hadn't done in a very long time. He laughed. Right there, in the middle of the Bylers' empty barn—he laughed until tears formed in his eyes.

Later, as he walked by Waneta's side, Mark's good mood was still intact. She, on the other hand, seemed to become more and more nervous. They'd hardly said a word to each other for the last ten minutes. However, he didn't think it was because she still feared him.

No, he was fairly certain it was because she was trying to save him from her parents' nosiness.

She was looking out for him. He'd tease her for being his defender if he wasn't so humbled by her intentions.

When they were about halfway to her house, she glanced up at him. "I suppose we should talk. I feel foolish walking without saying a word to each other."

"It's okay if you don't want to talk to me."

"Why is it okay? Do you not want to talk to me?"

He laughed. "Waneta, I'm walking by your side to your house. Obviously I don't mind talking with ya."

"My parents asked you to walk with me."

"I wouldn't be here if I didn't want to. You have to know that."

Looking sheepish, she smiled. "I do know that. You are a man with your own mind. I don't think you would ever do something you don't want to do."

"I've done plenty of things I didn't want to do. But this ain't one of them."

Her eyes widened at his blunt reply. "I never know how to respond when you say things like that."

"Say whatever you want, Waneta. I'm not going to get mad."

"When I'm with you, I feel all flustered. I don't know why."

He knew why. But he also wasn't willing to

rehash their differences in backgrounds again. Determined to make an effort, he blurted the first thing that came to mind. "Do you have a pet?"

"A pet?" She wrinkled her nose. "*Nee*. Why?"

"I don't know. I thought you probably had one. Most people have pets."

"Not me. Do you?"

"*Nee*." Now he was feeling flustered, too.

She smiled suddenly. "I guess most people have pets, except for the two of us."

He chuckled. "It would seem so. So, why don't you have one?"

"I don't know. I guess my family really ain't pet people." Looking a little defensive, she added, "A lot of people aren't, you know."

It was on the tip of his tongue to chide her for being so prickly. But then he remembered that he was attempting to build a conversation, not start an argument. "I was thinking of getting a dog," he blurted.

"You were?"

"Yeah." When he saw her raise her eyebrows, he asked, "Why are you acting so surprised?"

She pursed her lips. He thought he'd blown the conversation yet again. However, after a minute or so, she spoke. "I'm surprised only because I know that you work a lot. Dogs take a lot of time." She coughed. "I mean, I am assuming they do. What kind of dog do you want?"

He wasn't a liar, but he was starting to feel like one, since he'd actually never given what type of dog much thought. "It doesn't matter to me. I thought I'd go to the pound and see the dogs there."

"That will be so sad. They all need homes."

"I bet you're right," he said slowly. Just imagining dog after dog in cages, each one desperate to be let out, made a lump form in his throat. Why had he started this conversation anyway? "It will be hard to make a choice."

Blue eyes shining, Neeta added, "It's going to be wonderful-*gut*, though. Don'tcha think?" she asked, her tone wistful. "Mark, you will be rescuing a dog who needs a home."

Though she'd said his name before, she didn't say it often. Hearing his name on her tongue sounded good. "That will be wonderful. *Wunderbaar*." Impulsively, he said, "You should come with me."

"What?" Before he could take it back, she stopped and stared at him. "You really wouldn't mind me coming with you?"

He shook his head before he remembered that he hadn't actually planned to get a dog. "If you'd like to come, I'd be happy about that. I'm sure picking a dog will be a hard decision."

"You are going to need to find one who won't mind being home alone during the day. I think a big dog, too."

"Why big?"

"Because you're big." Her eyes widened. "I mean, um, I just assumed a man like you would want a sizable *hund*."

He chuckled at her expression. "I guess I had a big dog in mind." Then, because he couldn't seem to stop himself from digging his hole deeper, he found himself doing something he'd never done before. At least, not in recent memory, anyway. "Well, maybe we could go get one in a month or so. After I get the floors in my house fixed up."

"The nursery won't be as busy in another month. I could probably get a Friday or Saturday off in September or October. You, too."

Liking that they were making plans so far in advance, he nodded. "We'll pick a weekend when there isn't church. That way I'll have all Sunday to spend with it."

"That's a *gut* idea," she said as they walked up her front porch. "Mark, *danke* for asking me. It sounds like a lot of fun."

"What is going to be fun?" her father asked.

"Mark is going to adopt a *hund* from the shelter in a month or two. He asked me to go with him to pick it out."

Norman looked at him in surprise. "I see."

Mark felt his cheeks flush in embarrassment. "That is, if it is okay with you, Norman."

If anything, her father looked even more taken aback. "Well, now," he murmured. "I guess it is."

Still looking reflective, he said, "Neeta, go help your *mamm* in the kitchen for a few minutes. She's making iced tea and putting cookies on a tray for our guest."

"I feel bad about you going to so much trouble."

"It's no trouble at all, Mark," Norman said. "When people come over, my wife feeds them, whether they want to be fed or not."

"I'll be right back, Mark," Waneta said before walking into the house.

When they were alone, Norman gestured to one of the empty chairs that dotted the porch. "Have a seat and tell me about this dog you want."

"I, um, was just thinking about maybe getting a dog. I never intended to ask her to accompany me to the pound. It just kind of happened."

"That's the funny thing about our daughter. She inspires others to do all sorts of things they didn't intend to." Stretching his hands out in front of him, he chuckled. "You'd be amazed about the things she's encouraged me to do. Or maybe not."

"Like I said, if you'd rather me not take Waneta to the pound, I understand."

"You might understand. She would not. My daughter is a woman who doesn't change her mind."

"Yes, sir."

As if that settled that, Norman stretched his

legs and crossed his ankles. "So, how are things going for you?"

"Work is fine," he said carefully. "I like the nursery. I know Henry pretty well and am glad I can help him with some of the heavy lifting."

Looking satisfied, Norman nodded. "Henry is a *gut* man. He don't hire fools, either."

Since he was obviously referring to Henry having also hired his daughter, Mark said, "No, sir."

"And your *haus*? How goes it there?"

Mark knew Norman was looking for honesty, so he gave him that. "It's been difficult. It needs a lot of work. I'm currently ripping out the old linoleum flooring."

"Pulling out old linoleum ain't easy. It's a difficult undertaking."

"It is, but it will be worth it, I think. I discovered oak floors underneath in good repair. After I work on them a bit, they're going to be really fine. They'll make the whole place look better, too. Fresh."

Norman raised his eyebrows. "Fresh. *Jah*, I can see how that might be the case. Won't that be fine."

Feeling more eager and less like he was sitting for an interview, Mark nodded. "I believe so. When I made the decision to move back there, I knew I needed to make a lot of changes. My insides need it."

"I can understand that. You might not like me saying this, but I've often thought of you and your brother. You two had a hard time of it."

"We did." There was no reason to pretend otherwise.

"Was it difficult to make that choice to come back?"

"At first, no. Hearing that I could live somewhere rent free, it felt real good. But making my way back here was hard. That house was not a happy place. Not for me, not for any of us, really." Exhaling, he said, "But if I've learned anything, it's that the house is just that. A house. The memories hurt, but I don't want them to define me."

Norman eyed him steadily for a long moment before slapping his hands on his knees and standing up. "I'm *verra* glad you came over today, Mark. Mighty glad."

"I appreciated the invitation."

"Well, now. I think it's time I fetched Neeta. I imagine she's helped her mother enough for now."

After Norman departed, Mark sighed in relief. He felt as if he'd passed a test. He wasn't sure what Norman Cain had been hoping to discover that had been lurking inside of him, but it seemed that whatever he had been looking for, he'd found.

Unbidden, twin feelings of pride and embarrassment filled his insides. He'd been accepted. Deemed acceptable. That affirmation also left him feeling pretty embarrassed. He was twenty-six. Far too old to be needing acceptance from Waneta's father.

Far too old for it to feel so gratifying.

"Mark, are you all right?" Waneta asked. She had just stepped out on the porch. Two tall glasses of iced tea were in her hands.

He mentally shook his head. "Of course." Coming to his feet, he took one of the glasses from her. "Have you finished helping your mother already?"

She shrugged off the question. "Oh, that. Mamm and Daed wanted me out of the way so Daed could talk to you in private."

"I thought that might be what happened."

"Well, you thought right. I let Mamm know I wasn't happy about that, too. They shouldn't be inviting you over just to ask you pesky questions."

"You shouldn't have worried about it. I can take care of myself."

"Oh, I know that. But making you sit and talk with him the moment you got here was rude. I hope he didn't offend you too much? Or, if he did, I'll be glad to talk to him."

"There's no need for that," he assured her. He liked that she was attempting to be his protector. However, while he might seek acceptance like a child, he surely didn't want or expect anyone to fight his battles for him.

She sipped her drink. "Supper won't be ready for a little while. Would you like to play cards?"

"I guess so." Actually, he couldn't remember the last time he'd played.

"What about Rook? Is that okay?"

He hadn't played that game in years, not since he'd played with other teenagers on Sunday night singings and frolics. "I like it fine."

She breathed a sigh of relief. "I'm glad. I'll go get a deck of cards. We can stay here or go inside."

"Let's stay outside. It's warm, but not too bad under the shade."

"Okay. Great." He was starting to realize that her nervousness stemmed from him being a man and her a woman and not that she was afraid of him.

That made him want to gentle his voice and be even more patient with her. "Go find the cards. I'll be right here. Waiting for you."

Cheeks blooming, she darted back into the house. Chuckling to himself, he set the glasses on the worn table, then got up and walked to the porch railing.

It was warm out but pleasant enough. Surrounding the porch were a variety of shrubs and flowers. Boxwoods, burning bushes, and a crabapple tree decorated the bed on the right side. On the left were lavender, daisies, and black-eyed Susans. They were unpretentious flowers, he supposed. But bright and cheery, too. They reminded him of Waneta, a person who was easy and pretty on the outside, but whose sweet and caring personality shone through. He wondered if she was the gardener in the family. If so, then she was responsible for the well-tended beds. They flourished under her guidance.

He supposed he would probably transform the same way around her. Maybe some of his wildness would be tamed, too.

It was a fanciful thought. It amused him, too—realizing that he was hoping there really was something between him and Waneta. He would help her in any way that he could. And she? Well, she would give him the care and stability that he'd always craved.

Just as he was about to turn back to the table and sit down, he spied a movement near the edge of the Cains' property. Mark stepped forward, braced his hand on the railing, and stared more closely.

Spied a bright white shirt, then focused on the figure standing in the center of a grouping of pecan trees.

Mark was about to call out to Waneta that he was going to check on something when the man stepped out of the shadows of the trees and into the broad daylight.

Curious, Mark walked down the steps. As his eyes focused, he drew to a stop. Stunned. It was Calvin. His long-lost brother.

Mark stepped forward. Everything inside of him was crying out to go to Calvin. Hug him tightly. Promise anything so he wouldn't take off again.

But then a couple of things became apparent. Calvin was not Amish. The blinding white shirt was a T-shirt. It was untucked over a pair of dark jeans. His dark-brown hair was cut short, almost like a military buzz cut.

Calvin was also staring at him intently. His arms were crossed over his chest, his legs slightly parted. His chin was raised. He looked for all the world like he was daring Mark to acknowledge him.

Even from that distance, Mark could tell that there was nothing tentative about his brother's expression. It looked vaguely mocking. Derisive.

Almost taunting. Like he was daring Mark to come to him.

The door swung open then. "Sorry it took me so long," Waneta said in a rush. "I had quite the time finding two complete decks. Has that ever happened to you? Three of the card decks in our drawer were missing one or two cards. I couldn't believe it."

She was excited. Happy to play cards with him on the front porch. Here, at her house, where her parents had invited him to spend the afternoon with them. Where her mother was going to the trouble of making him supper.

This was his future if he wanted it. He could stay a little longer. Grab hold of Waneta Cain's goodness and her parents' acceptance into their life.

Or, he could make his excuses and go see his brother, who he'd once loved more than anything. The boy he'd tried so hard to protect but had failed. Who had never understood Mark, never even tried to understand his motivations for doing the things he had done. Who had left him and had never responded to his notes or calls. For years.

Who had come to find him, not at their house where they could sit and talk and try to figure things out. But at the Cains' residence. Lurking, too. Not even announcing himself and stepping forward. Stepping back into the community.

It was a hard decision. A difficult one.

But he knew what he had to do in order to survive.

Turning around, he smiled at Waneta. "I think everyone loses cards all the time," he murmured. "That's why card companies keep making more playing cards. Ain't so?"

Eyes bright, she smiled.

Mark loved her smile. Cherished it. If Waneta was his future and Calvin was his past, there was no choice. She represented everything he'd ever wanted.

Calvin? He was a reminder that everything he'd ever loved had caused him pain. He already knew what pain and rejection felt like. "You better deal," he said as he sat down next to her. "It's been so long since I've played, you're gonna have to walk me through the first game."

"I can do that. But eventually, you're going to be on your own. I'm a bit competitive when it comes to Rook, you see."

He laughed. "I'll pay close attention, then," he teased.

Though he still felt a prickling on the back of his neck, felt Calvin's unwavering gaze still watching him intently, Mark never looked out into the field again.

He didn't need to experience his past again to know that if he gave in, it would hurt.

Those memories were alive and well.

Chapter 10

Sunday, August 7

Calvin Fisher couldn't believe it. His own brother had just turned his back on him. Mark had looked him in the eye, then proceeded to pretend that he didn't exist.

After years and years of no communication, the first time Mark had seen him, he'd chosen to ignore him.

As that knowledge sunk in, Calvin stepped further into the shadows. He watched Mark sit down across from Waneta Cain, watched him lean back and relax. Just like he belonged at her house. Like he was comfortable there.

Across from him, Waneta was talking a mile a minute, all while fumbling with a deck of cards as she clumsily attempted to shuffle them. After dropping several on the ground, Mark bent down and picked them up. Then he reached for the remainder of them and proceeded to shuffle the deck neatly. As he did, Waneta gazed at him like he was doing something difficult. Then she said something to him that must have been extremely funny because Mark threw his head back and laughed.

Laughed! *Mark was laughing.* He was spending time with Waneta Cain, who everyone had thought was a cute girl but far too sheltered and sweet. Now she was an attractive woman and she had invited Mark into her home. And, from the way they were acting toward each other, it was apparent that he was courting her.

Courting, the Amish way.

The idea both sickened and amused him. His older brother was not only still Amish, he seemed to be thriving in the lifestyle. So much so, he'd decided to return to Horse Cave and claim their childhood home.

Even after everything they'd been through inside of those walls.

Calvin couldn't understand it, but then again, he'd never really understood how Mark thought. Mark was steady. He liked things to stay the same.

And he'd always been sure that his faith would save him and keep him from harm.

But it hadn't.

Calvin's body still bore plenty of scars and bruises from the many times God hadn't saved him from his father's anger or their mother's neglect.

From the time he'd reached eleven, Calvin had only been able to think about leaving Horse Cave. He couldn't wait to get far away from their dysfunctional parents. From their house that smelled like stale cigarettes and dust. From their slow-paced, backward way of life.

Not Mark. No matter how many times Calvin had talked to him about leaving together, even going as far as to list all the reasons why they should, his older brother had never agreed.

Calvin still remembered the day he'd cut his hair short, bought jeans and a pale blue T-shirt with the University of Kentucky insignia on it, and stared at himself in the mirror.

He'd looked different. In the new clothes, he'd felt different, too. Better. Almost taller. Definitely prouder.

Actually, he'd suddenly felt like he'd at last become the person he was meant to be. He'd felt like he'd suddenly had options. He could now be anyone he wanted. He could do things that had been forbidden. He could talk to people he wasn't supposed to.

He'd known then that whatever happened, his life could only get better. But instead of supporting his decision, Mark had yelled at him.

Said he was being stupid. Talked about how dangerous life was in the outside world. Like it wasn't dangerous in their own living room.

Being neglected and emotionally abused by two unhappy people had been awful. Going hungry and being cold in the winter had been miserable. Never knowing if their parents were going to be sober or drunk or high had been difficult, too.

But having a brother who refused to admit that their life was an essential tragedy had been painful as well. Calvin had needed him. But instead of getting support, Mark had only made excuses for their parents' actions.

He'd gotten so frustrated with him. Calvin wished that *he* was the older brother, that he'd have been able to shake Mark. To shake him so he would finally see reason.

Instead, all he'd ever gotten from Mark was another lecture.

It had been a difficult decision to come back to Horse Cave, but once he discovered that their father had died, he knew he no longer had anything to fear. Since then, he'd been driving through every couple of weeks, trying to come to terms with his past.

When he realized that Mark had moved in, he knew he had to do something. That house was half his, and he intended to make sure he got what was coming to him.

After looking around the place while Mark was out, he'd felt even more sure that he had made the right decision. The house was in better shape than he remembered. He was going to be able to get the money he needed out of it.

But now everything was messed up.

Finally, he made the decision to show himself

to Mark but was unable to find him. It had never occurred to him that he'd still be going to church.

So he'd waited. But when Mark didn't return home around noon, he'd gone looking for him. It was lucky that he'd run into Lora. She'd been only too happy to tell him that she'd seen Mark walking with Waneta toward her house.

So he'd stood outside and waited. Waited to be noticed.

When Mark met his gaze, Calvin almost felt like crying. After all these years, he was at last seeing the brother he'd depended on and had looked up to. Well, who he'd looked up to until it had become apparent that he wasn't ever going to put Calvin's needs first.

But what did Mark do?

He turned around and ignored him. Just like he didn't matter. Just like he wasn't worth anything.

Just like he'd done all those years ago.

Obviously, it was time to make a new plan. Reuniting with Mark and working together to put the house up for sale wasn't going to happen now.

Anger at the situation sliced through his very being. Why was life so hard? Why was it all so unfair?

Turning down the street, he walked back to his motorcycle. It was a late model Harley Dyna. It was banged up and more than a little scratched and worn, which was why he'd been able to afford it. It ran like a champ, though. Every time it roared to life, it gave him pleasure. It was a fitting symbol of how far his life had come from these quiet hills in central Kentucky.

Rubbing his hand along the fender, he felt a small sense of peace overtake him. Tonight, he would leave, head back to the cheap hotel he'd spied on the outskirts of Bowling Green, and figure things out. But first he decided to visit Lora again. He needed to be around someone who was just as out of place in Horse Cave as he was.

"What's wrong, Calvin?" Lora called out from her front porch. "And where's Mark? I thought you'd be all smiles right about now."

Turning, he took her in. Today, she had her hair up in some kind of complicated braid. Her black eyeliner made her blue eyes stand out; and her plain white tank top and snug low-riding jeans were no doubt causing most men in the area to give her a second glance.

But what drew him to her the most was the air of hope that continually surrounded her. He didn't understand it; she'd had as hard of a childhood as he had. She should seem a lot harder. Tougher.

Instead, it always seemed as if she was waiting for something good that was just around the corner. It was going to be a hard day when she realized that there wasn't anything like that.

Walking toward her, he smirked. He was hurting inside, but she didn't need to know that.

Watching him intently, she tilted her head to one side. "What happened?" In a rush she asked, "Oh! Did you not find the Cains' house? It's the one with the black door and the stone—"

There it was again. That optimism that she clung to. Feeling almost like he was letting her down, he cut her off. "No, I found it."

"Then, what's wrong? Why aren't you with him?" Before he could answer, she shot off another rapid question. "Oh. Were they not back from church yet?" The corners of her mouth turned up. "You know how some of those old folks are. They never want to leave . . ."

"They were there." Now that he'd answered her question, Calvin was tempted to turn around. Ignore all of her questions. Ride his Dyna, find a place to hole up for the night. He needed some time to figure out what to do next. If Mark was going to pretend he didn't exist and actually was planning to live in the house instead of selling it, then he was going to have to think of some way to encourage him to leave. He had no choice. He needed his half of the money from the sale of the house.

But as Lora continued to watch him, he was tempted to change his plans for the night. She was staring at him like he counted. She was looking at him in the exact opposite way that his own brother had stared at him. Lora was looking at him like she was sure he had something important to say.

He didn't know if he did or not. But he knew he liked her thinking that he did. He stepped forward.

If he couldn't count on his own brother, then he was going to need an ally in Hart County. While Lora continued to watch him, he walked up the steps of her front porch.

She stood there. Her lightly tanned arms crossed over that white tank, the toes of one of her bare feet curling against the beat-up wood floor.

When he didn't say anything for a couple more seconds, she raised her eyebrows. "Are you gonna tell me what happened, or are we just gonna stare at each other all afternoon?"

"They were back from church. All of them were," he said at last. "And Mark was there. I saw him standing on their front porch with Waneta."

"So, what happened? What did he say when he saw you? Did he run down to say hi?" Smiling, she said, "I bet he gave you a hug. Mark always used to do things like that."

He had. Mark had hugged him when he got hurt and scraped his knees. When they'd had no food in the house. When he'd had bad dreams at night. "No, we didn't hug."

"Well then, what happened?" Her eyes widened as she snapped her fingers. "Oh no. Did y'all already get in an argument? If you did, I bet he'll come around. Mark always put up with whatever you dished out. Ain't so?"

Her Kentucky accent, mixed in with such a typical Amish phrase, almost made him smile. "What if I told you that I don't want to talk about it?"

Disappointment flared in her expression, but she tamped it down. "Then I'd say that you don't have to."

"You mean that, don't you?"

"Yeah," she said quietly. "If you don't want to talk about something bad, then I'm the last person who's going to try to make you change your mind. I don't like to talk about my bad, either. I'll see you later."

Lora was expecting him to turn around and leave. But he was starting to think riding an hour away sounded like a lot of trouble, especially when he was going to need to come right back tomorrow. "Maybe I don't want to leave right now."

As if she sensed a new tension brewing between them, she gestured to the pair of metal chairs behind them. "If you don't have anywhere else to go, want to hang out with me for a while?"

He pushed off from the column he was leaning against but didn't sit down. "What do you have in mind?"

Her body tensed. "Nothing. I thought we could just talk or something."

"I could do that . . . if you have something to drink. Got anything?"

"I got a couple of cans of beer."

Just as she moved to the door, he added, "You got anything else?" She was pretty, but if he was going to be dealing with his brother ignoring him, he was going to need a whole lot more than just a couple of cans of beer to get him through the night.

She frowned. "There might be an old bottle of tequila. I gotta check. I don't drink much anymore."

"Good thing I have some weed, then. You up for that?"

Lora shrugged. "Maybe."

"Maybe?"

"I haven't done that in a while, either." She stared at him closely. "You're upset about Mark, aren't you?"

"Not really," he said, though she spied some hurt in his eyes. "What's wrong with you? You don't look real happy to see me."

"Nothing's wrong. I just didn't plan on spending my afternoon like this."

"What did you plan on doing?" He smirked. "Bible study?"

After a short pause, she opened her screened door. "Of course not."

"Then what's the problem? I mean, it ain't like you've got any other friends coming over, right?"

A new shadow filled her gaze. "Right. Come on in and I'll show you around."

Calvin had no interest in seeing her house. All he wanted to do was forget things for a while. But since Lora was looking like she wanted to talk, not just hang out, he shrugged. "Yeah, sure. Show me around, Lora. Can't wait."

When Lora closed the door shut behind them and locked it, effectively shielding them from the rest of the world, Calvin Fisher finally relaxed.

This wasn't what he'd planned to do today, but it was better than hurting.

It was better than a lot of things he'd done.

Chapter 11

T his is going to be a nice change, ain't so?" Waneta asked Mark when he joined her at the outside checkout stand, just in front of the row of four greenhouses at Blooms and Berries. "I'm glad Mr. Lehmann asked us to work out here together. Usually, I man the cash register while you stock and carry."

Mark grinned. "I'm pleased about it, too, though also worried that you might get sick of me. I'm such a talker, you know."

She playfully nodded, since there was no doubt which one of them was the real conversationalist. "I might need to ask for earplugs or something so I can hear myself think."

"I'll try not to irritate you for a couple hours yet."

"I think you might be irritating me right now," she said with a wink. Then, realizing how mean that sounded, she said quickly, "You know I'm only joking, right?"

"Of course. You wouldn't hurt a fly on purpose." Looking pleased, he added, "I'm glad that you feel you can joke around with me now. It's fun."

"I think so, too." Actually, she was finding that spending time with Mark was always nice. They were becoming good friends. It was a pleasant surprise.

And, if she sometimes thought of him in some way other than just as a friend . . . well, he hopefully would never find out.

As Mark watched still more people park in the lot, he said, "Have you worked many of Henry's sidewalk sales?"

"Oh, *jah*. At least five or six. Mr. Lehmann holds two a year."

"What can you tell me about them?"

Thinking about the crowds of people that seemed to come in waves, each demanding seedlings as quickly as possible, she murmured, "Just be prepared. They're really popular and sometimes people ask for more than you can give."

"So I need to be prepared to let them down easily."

"*Nee*, you need to be prepared to be firm. Mr. Lehmann has a limit of no more than seven seedlings per person. Make all the customers stick to that."

"I'll do my best."

She almost giggled. Mark Fisher was a formidable presence. She might be becoming more comfortable around him, but that wasn't exactly the case with everyone in the county. She'd noticed at church on Sunday that while people were more cordial, they definitely were watching him with distant expressions. They still didn't completely trust him.

That made her think that people weren't going to argue with him.

Of course, everyone might not want to even come up to the counter if he was there. And that could be a problem. Mr. Lehmann would lose business.

And how would Mark react to that? Not very well, she guessed. Maybe even worse than not well. Maybe he would even get really angry.

Then what would she do?

"Waneta?"

"I'm sorry. My mind drifted off." Pasting on a reassuring smile, she said, "Mark, please, don't worry about a thing. Everyone from all over Hart County comes for plantings and seeds. It makes the day go by fast."

"I can handle that. Thanks for letting me know what to expect."

Realizing that he didn't look all that happy, whether it was because of the change in routine or for some other reason, Neeta felt some of her earlier exuberance and optimism dim. "Do you want to work the register or bag?"

"It don't matter to me, Waneta."

"Why do you always call me by my full name?"

"I like it."

"That's the reason?"

"It's a good one, don't you think?"

"I suppose." She was starting to feel even more and more confused. "Though, I prefer *Neeta*. Hardly anyone calls me Waneta."

"I'll be different, then."

She smiled weakly. "*Jah*."

"You ready?" Mr. Lehmann called out. "I'm about to tell Ben to open the gates."

"We're ready," Mark answered.

"*Gut*. Off we go." Mr. Lehmann raised his voice as he moved the little walkie-talkie close to his mouth. "Ben, open 'em up!"

Almost immediately, they heard cars pull forward in one gate and other folks walk through another gate that Ben had propped open.

Every person who strode forward seemed to have a mission in mind. They darted to and fro, inspecting seedlings and grabbing some of the small mini carts that Blooms and Berries kept for just this occasion. One of Mr. Lehmann's older employees was walking around and helping folks make decisions.

Less than five minutes later, they had their first customers at the counter. Waneta felt her stomach clench, half waiting for the two Mennonite women to refuse Mark's assistance.

But they purchased their items easily and even chatted with Mark while doing it.

Once they turned away with cheery waves, Mark leaned toward her. "It's going to be okay, Waneta. No one is going to be mean. But even if they are, I'll be able to handle it."

"You shouldn't have to, though. It ain't right."

"It isn't something that I can't handle. Besides, I knew what it would be like when I moved back here. I knew some people would have a real hard time with me being here."

"I just want to kick some people in the shin when they are rude to you, though. We are supposed to forgive . . . and there isn't even anything to forgive. You were proven innocent."

Mark looked like he was going to say something more, but two men and a pair of women walked up.

And so it began.

For the next several hours, she and Mark rang people up, bagged or boxed their purchases, and helped customers. Mr. Lehmann offered to take their places at the counter so each could take a lunch, but by mutual agreement, neither wanted to leave the other.

The most Waneta was willing to do was run to take a quick bathroom and water break.

By three o'clock, the nursery was like a ghost town. Everyone who had wanted something specific had gotten what they'd wanted.

"You two did a real good job," Mr. Lehmann

said. "You didn't even take any breaks, either. I'm obliged."

"I was glad to help, Henry," Mark said. "Now, how about you go home for the day? I can clean everything up."

"That ain't necessary."

"You hired me so you wouldn't have to work so hard. Let me help you."

"I'll stay and help, too, Mr. Lehmann," Waneta said with a smile. "We've got this."

But instead of agreeing, their boss fidgeted. "I'm afraid you are needed somewhere else, son." After a pause, he gestured toward the empty parking lot. "The sheriff just called me on my cell phone. He's on his way over. He . . . well, he wants to talk to you."

Mark nodded, but his face had become perfectly blank.

Waneta knew he was taken aback. She was, too. "Why does Sheriff Brewer need to speak with him?" she asked. "He's been working here beside me the whole time."

"I know, Neeta."

"Then what does he want?"

"Don't worry," Mark murmured. "I'll be okay."

"You keep saying that, but I don't believe it. And now look—the sheriff is bothering you for no reason."

"Settle down, Waneta," Mr. Lehmann said.

"No one is in trouble. You are jumping to conclusions."

Realizing he was right, she nodded.

"It looks like he just arrived. What do you think I should do? Wait here or go over to meet him?" Mark asked.

Mr. Lehmann sighed. "Looks like he made the decision. He's walking over toward us right now."

Looking resigned, Mark started walking. "I'll meet him halfway."

"I'm sure it will go all right," Mr. Lehmann said.

Waneta felt so helpless. Mark looked like he had the weight of the world on his shoulders and didn't expect anyone to lend a hand. "I'll wait for you after we clean up," she called out.

"Don't," he said, his voice flat. "There's no telling how long this will take."

"I don't mind waiting." Trying to sound encouraging, she said, "Why, I bet the sheriff just has a question about your house or something."

But instead of seeming to make him feel better, he flinched. "I don't want you to wait, Waneta. No offense, but I'd rather not be talking to the sheriff while you are staring at us from across the way."

She was kind of offended. "I'm not going to just stand around and stare at you."

"Please, just help Henry clean up and then go on home."

"I can handle anything, and I want to help. To be there for you. I know I'm only a small-town girl who has been pretty sheltered, but I am stronger than I look."

He didn't hear her. He'd already walked away. Watching his back, she felt so hurt. After everything she'd been doing, how could Mark still not trust her?

"Listen to him, child," Mr. Lehmann said.

"But I don't want him to feel so alone. He doesn't have to tackle everything all by himself."

"Let him have some pride, Waneta," he whispered.

"There's nothing wrong with trying to help a friend," she countered. "And I am his friend."

"I'm glad you are. I can tell that he's thankful for it, too. But getting in the middle of this won't help him. He's going to be embarrassed if you discover whatever the sheriff is going to talk to him about."

"I'm not going to judge him," she blurted.

Looking over her shoulder, it was evident that Mark was in a deep, serious conversation with the sheriff. Both of their stances were rigid and whatever they were talking about looked intense. "Something bad must have happened," she whispered. "I wonder what Sheriff Brewer is telling him." A new idea struck her then. "Or, do you think he's talking to Mark about his past again?"

Mr. Lehmann looked concerned. "Waneta, here's the thing. Everyone needs to keep some secrets to themselves. He doesn't want you knowing about his past. He doesn't want you knowing about the sheriff talking to him. Let it go."

Not wanting to go against both Mark's and her boss's instructions, Waneta stepped backward. "If that's the way you feel, I think I had better just go on home."

His expression gentled. "Good, child. Yes, go home, and don't you worry about Mark none. Everything will turn out in due time."

Waneta supposed Mr. Lehmann had wanted to make her feel better with his words. But all they did was leave her feeling empty, like she had only been half filled with information. What, exactly, did he mean "in due time"? Was he thinking of a week? A month? Years?

Though of course he could have no idea what the future held for them, she had to admit that she was uneasy about how nebulous it was. She needed something to hold on to.

Turning, she grabbed her purse and the lunch she'd never eaten and walked as quickly as she could toward the main gates. The pace she was going at made her perspire, making the dark-pink dress she was wearing stick to her back.

When she was just a few feet away, she couldn't help herself and looked over at Mark and Sheriff Brewer one last time. They were in deep discussion. Mark did not look happy and the sheriff looked serious and grim.

While it didn't seem as if Mark was in trouble, it was evident that something serious had happened that affected him.

Taking a peek at Mark again, she saw him flinch. His expression turned from serious to ravaged. He was in pain.

Something awful had happened. But from the way he'd treated her questions, she feared that he'd never share it with her.

If that was the case, it left her feeling like her heart was breaking. Because how could she ever believe in a man who kept so much of his life closed to himself?

How could she ever have a real relationship with Mark if he refused to talk about whole parts of his life? If he didn't trust her to support him, she wondered if there would be other situations in the future that he might try to keep hidden from her.

She hoped and prayed she was wrong. That she was overreacting and that her inexperience in relationships was making her doubt things.

But if she was right? Well, she was going to have to resign herself to only being his friend. She couldn't give her heart to a man who was so wary.

At least, she didn't think she could.

Chapter 12

Monday, August 8

Sheriff Brewer looked uncomfortable, shifting from one foot to the other. He pulled out a white handkerchief from a back pocket and mopped his brow. Then, at last, he continued. "So that is the reason I wanted to talk to you about this, Mark."

"Because you saw my brother, and you know that he's gotten into some trouble in the past."

"It is more than just a bit of trouble. He assaulted Lora Weaver last night before taking off."

Mark clenched his hands as shame coursed through him. Once again he was getting pulled into a family member's crimes and mistakes and he was feeling compelled to fix them. But how could he fix this?

"Is Lora going to be all right?" he asked quietly.

"I think so. She didn't want any medical attention. My deputy told me that she looks bad but should recover in a day or two."

"I am sorry that she got hurt. I hate that Calvin was the cause of it, too," he said haltingly. "I don't know what to say. I didn't even know they were still friends."

"I don't know what their relationship is. All I do know is that he was at her house partying the other night."

"Partying?"

Sheriff Brewer looked at his notes. "When Deputy Beck entered Lora's house, it was obvious that she and Calvin had been smoking pot. The place was also littered with beer cans, too."

"I'm not saying that what they were doing was right, but it kind of sounds like you are pretty upset about something that two people over twenty-one are doing. Smoking marijuana is a pretty small crime, compared to some other things that have been going on around here."

"I agree. But it is still a crime. Assaulting her is a crime as well."

"Yes. Yes, of course."

The sheriff continued. "Deputy Beck searched the house. Lora was pretty emphatic that they weren't her drugs. That Calvin had brought them to her."

"I'm sorry to hear this. I haven't talked to him in years. I've heard rumors that he's gotten into some trouble, but I don't know the extent of it."

Sheriff Brewer scanned his notes again. "Hmm. Looks like Calvin has been arrested several times for drug and alcohol charges in

Ohio, Kentucky, and Indiana." Looking at his phone he murmured, "Though it seems he's been questioned about some other matters."

Other matters. Mark felt his stomach sink.

Calvin had made a mess of his life. It was also obvious that he wasn't planning to change his ways. Not from what he'd seen from a distance, at least. Feeling irritated and angry at the whole situation, Mark wondered about the timing of it all.

Why had Calvin decided to show up barely two weeks after he'd arrived back in Horse Cave? It wasn't like they had anything to do with each other. Not in years.

And what had he been doing with Lora Weaver? Mark had been under the impression that she was working at Bill's Diner and trying to get her life back on track. Was that rumor wrong, too?

But even that didn't explain why Sheriff Brewer had taken it upon himself to come talk to Mark about it in the middle of his workday. In front of half the town. It was almost like he had done it on purpose in order to sabotage all of Mark's efforts to fit in and be accepted in the community.

The worst of it was that Waneta had watched with worry in her eyes. It felt like all the progress they'd made had been erased and they were back where they'd started.

He hated that. He resented Calvin's interference, too. And the sheriff's visit to his place of work. Lashing out, he said, "You know I wasn't with Lora and Calvin, Sheriff. I wasn't at her house doing drugs. And as much as it pains me to say this, what Calvin does is no business of mine. I ain't my brother's keeper."

Sheriff Brewer nodded easily, like he completely understood. And, unfortunately, like he had nothing but time on his hands. After taking care to fold his handkerchief neatly again, he said, "Any idea why he's back here?"

"None. Like I said, I haven't talked to him in years." Unable to stop himself, he glanced over toward Waneta. She wasn't looking his way anymore. Instead, she was in deep conversation with Henry. It looked serious. "You already know this. We talked at length about my family when you took me in for questioning for Bethany two years ago."

"People change. I thought maybe he had."

"If he did, he didn't tell me. I have not seen him."

"At all?"

That moment flashed back in his mind. Of sitting on Waneta's porch. Of her quietly flirting with him. Then, of him glancing up and seeing Calvin staring at him.

And Calvin staring at Waneta.

It had taken everything he'd had to not go over to Calvin and yell at him to go away.

He'd kept a tight lid on his self-control. If he

hadn't, he would have opened himself to being hurt again—allowing himself hope that Calvin would want to see him again; that his brother might say he missed him. Or that he wanted to get to know him again.

Or that he'd wanted to say he was sorry for the things he'd done.

But Mark's heart, which had been stomped on too many times, guided him that day.

"I did see him recently. Yesterday. However, we didn't talk."

Sheriff Brewer's expression sharpened. "What happened?"

"I saw him from a distance." Haltingly, he added, "I think he wanted me to stop what I was doing and rush over to talk to him."

"But you didn't?"

Mark shook his head. "I ignored him. Turned away. The next time I looked up, he was gone." That was almost the truth, anyway.

"Where were you, if you don't mind me asking?"

Sheriff Brewer was a master at asking questions in that slow, Kentucky drawl. He could look humble and sleepy while asking difficult and uncomfortable questions. Against his will, Mark felt his skin start prickling and his upper back start sweating.

"I was at Waneta Cain's *haus*," he said. Not because he wanted to share where he was, but because he knew he had no choice. Sheriff Brewer would find out anyhow.

"So she could vouch for you?"

"Vouch for what? I went to church on Sunday morning, then spent several hours with Waneta and her family that afternoon."

"And after that?"

"After that, I didn't do anything special. I just went home."

"Could Waneta or her parents vouch for seeing him as well?"

This was turning painful. So uncomfortable, he was wondering if he should be asking if he needed a lawyer. "I don't think any of them saw him," Mark said slowly. "Calvin was lurking near a cove of trees. He didn't want to be seen." Well, not by anyone but him.

Sheriff Brewer's expression brightened. "Lurking, you say?"

"Like I just said, Calvin didn't want to be seen by Waneta or her parents," Mark said, each word now tinged with frustration. "Only by me."

"Why do you think that is?" asked the sheriff.

"I don't know." Feeling even more frustrated, he said, "Look, I don't understand why you are asking me all of these questions or why you've chosen to talk to me here. Do you not trust me? Are you trying to make sure everyone here doesn't forget about my past?"

"None of those things." After the sheriff wiped

his brow again, he stuffed the white handkerchief in a back pocket. "I was hoping for your help, that's all . . ."

"I would help if I could. I haven't kept up with Lora or Calvin, but even I had heard that she'd changed. The things you are saying are disturbing."

"I think so, too. She swore up and down that the drugs were his. If that's the truth, then I want to talk to him."

"Which is the real reason you are here," Mark said.

"I am. Drugs are a bad enough problem in Hart County without someone new coming in and bringing more. If he's bringing Lora pot, he could be bringing much worse to other people in the county. I aim to put a stop to it."

Mark swallowed. This conversation was getting worse and worse. Now he was not only worried about his reputation, but he was concerned about his brother . . . and how Calvin would feel if Mark had to be the one to catch him and bring him in. "If I see him, I'll let you know."

Sheriff Brewer visibly relaxed. "Thank you. I'm sorry to come here to see you, but I honestly didn't think you'd have a problem with it. I only wanted some answers as quickly as possible."

"So, you still believe I am innocent of Bethany's assault?"

The sheriff looked at him curiously. "Of course

I do. I wouldn't have let you go if I wasn't a hundred percent sure you had nothing to do with it, Mark. I don't *believe* you are innocent, I *know* you are." After glancing in Henry's direction and tipping his hat, he said, "I came here to get answers. That's all."

Mark looked in the man's eyes and saw complete honesty there. The sheriff was telling the truth and asking him for help. And because of that, he knew what he needed to do. "I'll help you if I can. Calvin may be my brother by birth, but we don't mean much to each other anymore," he said, though he feared that wasn't the truth. "I want to stay here. I care about this community, too. I aim to settle in, marry one day and have children here. I don't want it to be a place where I'm worried about my brother hitting women or peddling drugs."

"I appreciate it." After handing him his card, he said, "Take this and call me if you find out anything. Anything at all."

"Yeah. Sure," Mark said.

After Mark stood and watched the sheriff's vehicle disappear, he walked back to Henry, who was standing alone at the checkout counter. "I'm sorry about that."

"Everything all right?" Henry asked.

"*Jah.*" He was tempted to say something more, but how could he? Waneta was just beginning to trust him. If he did say more, and Henry inadvertently told Waneta that Mark had seen Calvin creeping around her property, watching her and him, it would ruin every bit of the trust he'd gained from her over the last week.

"Though it ain't my business, I hope Sheriff Brewer was being fair with ya."

"He was." Clearing his throat, Mark added, "He had some questions about my brother."

"Calvin?"

"*Jah*. He fears Calvin has returned to Hart County."

Henry's brows furrowed. "*Fears* seems like a pretty strong word to describe a brother's return."

"It's fitting, though. I'm afraid he hasn't changed much over the years."

Henry's gaze sharpened. "You sound as if you know that for a fact. Do you?"

"*Nee*. I am only saying that because of what the sheriff said." That sense of unease he'd experienced earlier returned. Was he now being too cautious? Was he now judging Calvin based on a couple of rumors . . . just like so many people in the area judged him?

Henry's expression didn't smooth, but Mark didn't have any more time to worry about that because several customers came up needing help all at the same time.

Later, as he rang up one customer's seedlings and another's fruits and vegetables, Henry chatting with each one as if they were long-lost friends, Mark began to feel like he'd just made a terrible mistake.

Unfortunately, he wasn't sure who he'd just made that mistake with. Was it with the sheriff, Henry, or Waneta?

Or, maybe, it was with his brother. What if Calvin had changed after all?

What if he'd come to find him and had hoped that Mark would help him in some way? What if he hadn't wanted a thing, he'd only wanted to reconnect and Mark had turned his back on him? And then, feeling bad because his brother hadn't given him the time of day, Calvin had sought Lora Weaver out?

A slow line of dread filled him at the thought. Here, he'd been so upset and felt betrayed because he'd wanted the community to give him another shot. To give him a chance to prove that he was worth more than they'd ever believed him to be. What if he had done the very same thing to his little brother?

He hoped that wasn't the case. But if it was, he feared he had just made a terrible mistake that he was going to be paying for in the days and weeks to come.

Chapter 13

Monday Evening

I don't understand why you think we need to talk again," Lora said as she led Sheriff Brewer and Deputy Beck to the screened porch located at the back of her house. "I haven't done anything wrong."

"Other than create a public disturbance and smoke pot?" Sheriff Brewer asked with more than a small amount of sarcasm in his tone.

Glad her back was to him, Lora grimaced. She hated that she'd messed up yet again. Though she now lived the majority of her days in a way she was proud of, she still sometimes slipped. She certainly had Sunday night.

That said, she wasn't sure why her actions necessitated not one but two visits from the sheriff. It seemed a little excessive. Because of that, she was worried. They knew something she didn't, putting her at a disadvantage.

But showing weakness wasn't going to help anything. It hadn't when she was a little girl, and it hadn't when she'd been living on her own in northern Kentucky. Her only option was to brazen it out. Otherwise, these men would continue to view her as weak and maybe even try to take advantage of her.

As they entered the cool and comfortable screened porch, she looked over her shoulder at them. "First of all, we already discussed this. I've apologized for causing a disturbance. And the pot is gone. You know that." Focusing on the deputy, she hardened her voice. "You walked through the whole place even though I said several times that I didn't have any in the house. After I told you again and again that it wasn't mine."

"You're right. The house was clear," the deputy murmured.

Honestly, the deputy sounded as if he had suspected there was a meth lab down in the basement. Huh. It seemed he thought even less of her than she'd imagined. She sighed. "You know what? If we were in Washington State or Colorado, a Baggie of pot wouldn't be a concern."

"But we aren't there, are we?" Deputy Beck asked.

Wincing, she closed her eyes. For some reason, hearing the derision in the deputy's voice hurt even worse than hearing it from the sheriff.

Probably because Deputy Eddie Beck looked so composed and perfect. He had a lanky build and tanned arms. His hair was bleached from the sun. She remembered hearing something at the diner about him being really outdoorsy. He liked to camp and hike, and fish and ski. He had clear light-green eyes and an easy smile. All the girls at Bill's fanned themselves when they saw him walk inside. He smiled and charmed them all. Not her, though.

No, he wasn't smiling at all. Instead, he was examining her in a professional way. Like she was a witness to a crime. Or a piece of evidence he needed to transport to the lab.

He was eyeing her exactly the way he had late last night, like she was simply one more person he had to talk to as part of his job.

Seeing his expression made her squirm inside. All of her bad decisions from over the last few years came rushing back. She'd thought the recent changes she'd made might have balanced them out, but they didn't.

Not at all. At least not to him. Had she come this far just to be viewed as a loser girl all over again? After gesturing for them to have a seat on one of the brightly colored chairs that her sister Amanda and her husband had purchased before moving away, she decided to throw out all her ideas of acting cool and aloof.

She was too scared and too nervous to put on an act. She also had too much to lose. She needed to be as open and honest with the sheriff and his deputy as she possibly could.

Once she also sat down in the comfy chair, she

said, "What has happened? Did something else happen that I haven't heard about?"

"We'll talk about that, Lora. But first, how are you feeling?" Sheriff Brewer asked.

She shrugged. "All right."

"Your bruises look worse," Deputy Beck murmured. "Are you in pain?"

She was hurting, but it wasn't anything she couldn't handle. She pressed a palm to her bruised and swollen cheek. "I'm all right."

Shifting, he pulled out his phone. "Want me to find you a doctor? I can take you."

Lora was shocked. He was acting as if he cared about her. They both were. "I don't need a doctor. Like I told you last night, my face hurts, but my pride hurts worse."

The deputy stiffened. "Your pride? Why? Are you embarrassed?"

"Well, yes."

"You have nothing to be embarrassed about. Calvin Fisher is at fault. Only him. *Not you,*" he added with emphasis. "He shouldn't have raised a hand to you. There is no scenario where that is okay."

He sounded so sure, so emphatic, she wasn't certain how to respond. Clearing her throat, she said, "Is that the reason y'all stopped by? Because you were interested to see how I was feeling?"

"No," Deputy Beck said.

After exchanging a look with each other, Sheriff Brewer spoke. "Lora, here's the deal. We know you had Calvin over here. We know you had your own little party. We know you fought and he hit you. And we know he left soon after." His voice hardened. "But what we don't know is where he is now."

"Like I told you last night, I don't know where Calvin is either."

"You positive about that?" Deputy Beck asked.

She hated this so much. Had they only pretended to care so she'd lower her guard? "I'm very positive." When his expression didn't change, she threw the remains of her composure on the floor. "Deputy Beck, it's obvious that you don't think very highly of me. I know we have completely different backgrounds. I know I've made a lot of mistakes in my life. I know I've even done things you would never even think about doing. But that doesn't make me a liar."

"I didn't say you were."

"It's pretty obvious that you don't believe me."

"It's not that I don't believe you, it's that I don't know what to believe." He flushed. "Cases like this are hard for me. I get too emotionally involved. I can't help it, though. I hate men who beat up girls."

"Even girls like me?" she whispered. Because she had heard it before. After she'd run away, she'd found herself in a whole lot of bad areas, surrounded by lots of people who were used to breaking rules. She'd gotten hurt before. Once, even bad enough to have to go to the emergency room.

But even there, the orderlies and nurses seemed to judge her. They'd stopped short of saying she got what she deserved, but they insinuated it.

Looking even more frustrated, the deputy sighed. "Lora—may I call you that?" When she nodded, he continued. "What I think about you has no bearing on us trying to do our job."

"Actually, I think it has everything to do with that. Everyone here in Horse Cave only sees me as the girl from the bad home who never made anything of herself."

"I'm not from here. I don't know about your past and I don't—"

She cut him off. "But I am trying to get better," she blurted, even though it was probably way more than either of the men cared about. "I got my GED. I even got some counseling when I lived up near Covington. So, even though I'm still making mistakes, I'm better than I was."

"Lora," Sheriff Brewer said slowly, "about last night—"

"I don't know why I messed up so badly. I guess I was feeling so bad about myself that I didn't feel like arguing when Calvin wanted to get high."

And just like that, she felt stupid all over

again. Here she'd been asking them to see her as someone worthy of respect, as a woman who was working hard to turn her life around, but the proof was in her actions.

"So you joined him."

"Yeah, I did. But that doesn't mean I'm going to do that tonight or tomorrow or next week. I want to change." Thinking she sounded weak, Lora hardened her tone. "No, *I will change.*"

"Lora," Sheriff Brewer began, "you aren't in trouble. We came here to talk about Calvin."

"And I told you that I don't know where he is, Sheriff Brewer. Until he showed up in town a few days ago, I hadn't seen him in years. When he showed up, I was feeling kind of down. Though I knew better, I invited him in. It was a big mistake. Before long, we'd had too much to drink and started arguing about stupid things."

"Like what?"

"Like my sisters," she said impatiently. "Like his brother, Mark. Like a volleyball game we'd played in sixth grade. Then, when it was more than obvious that we don't have anything in common, that I don't even like him, I told him to leave." Releasing a ragged sigh, she tried to regain her composure. "And that is when he hit me," she said quietly. "He hit me because he said I was putting him down. Maybe I was."

"If you see him again, will you let us know?" Sheriff Brewer asked.

"Sure."

As the men stood up, the sheriff's phone rang. "I've got to get this. Meet me at the station," he said to the deputy.

"Sure, Pat." Turning to Lora, Deputy Beck said quietly, "I like my job. I really do. But I hate when I cause people to get so upset. Sorry about that."

He was apologizing? "It's all right. You are just doing what you have to do."

He nodded as they continued their short journey to the front door. "Hey, there's something else I've been meaning to ask you."

"What?"

"How come you never wait on me when I go to Bill's?"

Because he was too cute. Because she hated that she noticed that he was so cute. "Have I not waited on you? Huh. I thought I had."

"You haven't. I would have remembered."

"Ah."

"Next time I come in, if you are working, can I sit in your section?"

She was nodding before she even realized it. "Okay."

"Thanks." Smiling at her, he said, "I'm looking forward to having a regular conversation with you."

Smiling weakly, she opened the door. "I guess I'll see you at Bill's, then."

"Hope so." He smiled again, before walking to his vehicle.

Leaving her feeling more than a little tongue-tied and befuddled.

Chapter 14

Wednesday, August 10

Two days had passed since Waneta watched Mark have an intense conversation with Sheriff Brewer; two days after Mark essentially informed her that his business was none of her concern. She wasn't going to lie—hearing those words had hurt.

She thought they were friends. After he'd come over and they'd spent hours playing cards together, she felt that they were becoming closer, that he was feeling the same spark that she was.

But it looked like she was wrong.

Yesterday, she'd tried to encourage Mark to reach out to her. She teased and cajoled. She smiled and reminded him of how nice it had been to have him at her home. She was willing to do just about anything to get him to gaze at her in that warm, trusting way again. But nothing seemed to work.

Actually, all her references seemed to make him even more distant.

Therefore, in an effort to shield her heart, she was stepping back. Maybe she'd been wrong about him. Maybe he wasn't simply scarred from his childhood and being unjustly questioned. Or, maybe, it was something simpler than that. Maybe he simply didn't like her as much as she liked him.

All she did know was that she was tired of trying to convince Mark Fisher that she was worth his time and trust. It was time to treat him as she would anyone else. Like a coworker. Nothing more, nothing less.

Ironically, her new attitude caught his attention on Tuesday. He seemed confused by it. More than once he tried to talk to her about her sudden coolness toward him. He looked hurt when she didn't immediately smile and act like they were best friends—which just made her more irritated. Was he playing a game with her?

She even briefly wondered if everyone else had been right and she'd been wrong. What if he had beaten up Bethany after all? What if he was capable of forming friendships, then randomly breaking ties with the ease of breaking bread?

If so, then she'd been a fool.

Now, this morning, just as she was getting ready for work, her parents decided to jump into the fray.

"When is Mark going to come over again?" Daed asked when he'd joined her at the kitchen table. "Have you asked him over for supper yet?"

"*Nee.*"

"Why ever not? We asked you to."

"I know, Daed." She sipped her coffee and pretended to be concerned about her list in front of her of things to do.

But instead of taking the hint, Daed only frowned. "Waneta, I told you that we liked Mark. Mamm and me like him a lot." Smiling slightly, he added, "The man was good company for me, too. He doesn't act as if my mind is as far gone as my body. Not everyone sees that, you know."

What could she say to that? She didn't want to hurt her father's feelings or his waning social life. But she had to guard her heart. "Daed, as a matter of fact . . . Mark and I realized that we don't have much to say to each other anymore."

"How can that be? You two talked like magpies on Sunday."

Picking up her pencil, she crossed off another item on her list. "Things change, Daed. I think we're simply going to be work friends for now."

Her mother frowned as she bustled around the kitchen. When she walked over to pour Waneta's glass of orange juice, she said, "Neeta, I watched the two of you playing cards on the front porch."

"Mamm, you were standing at the window?"

"I'm not going to apologize for caring. Not especially when I watched Mark smile at you."

Her voice softened. "It was a sweet smile, daughter. A tender one. It was obvious that he didn't just want to be your friend. He wanted to be more than friends with you."

That reminder stung. But so did his change of heart. "Just because he wants something more doesn't mean I do. It takes two, you know."

"I agree. But it also takes a willingness to want to get to know someone better. Ain't so?" her mother asked as she fussed in front of the oven again. "Neeta, if you two got in a little argument, you need to stop being so stubborn and get over it."

"Mamm, just a week ago, you were gossiping about him."

"That is true, and I feel badly about that," she said as she fussed with the edge of her apron. "I've done a lot of praying. And I took Preacher Eli's sermon to heart."

"We both did," Daed added. "You should, too."

Waneta barely refrained from rolling her eyes. "I hear what you're saying, but I can't live my life according to Preacher Eli's wishes."

"You should, though. Mark is a good man," Daed said. "Give him another chance. He needs a person like you in his life."

"I did give him my friendship. It wasn't a good decision, though."

"Why not?" her mother called out as she fried bacon. "What happened?"

This was really too much of a conversation to have first thing in the morning. But the timing was as much her fault as anyone's. All week, she'd changed topics every time her parents brought up his name.

After taking a fortifying sip of juice, she said, "I think he has secrets, Mamm. A lot of secrets." *There.* That should give her parents an understanding about Mark.

But instead of looking concerned, her mother chuckled. "Well, of course he does."

"Don't you find that a bit of a red flag?"

"Not so much. If you already knew everything about him, you two wouldn't have anything to learn about each other."

She was talking as if they were already a couple. They were absolutely not. "I don't want to be in a relationship with a man whom I canna trust."

Her father frowned. "Something happened that you didn't tell us."

"You're right. Something did."

"Now would be a good time to share, child."

She knew that tone well. It was too ingrained in her not to respond accordingly. "On Monday, right toward the end of the sidewalk sale, Sheriff Brewer came to Blooms and Berries. He looked serious and asked to talk to Mark privately. And when I tried to talk to Mark about it, he pushed me away. He said there was nothing for me to worry about. That it was his business, not mine."

Silence met her statement.

She swallowed. It was too bad that she had to burst their bubble, but she supposed she couldn't shield them from distressing news all the time. "Now do you see why I need to keep my distance?"

"I can see how it must have been an awkward moment," Mamm said. "I bet poor Mark was embarrassed!"

Wait a minute. Poor Mark?

Shoving a plate in front of her, Mamm said, "Here. Have a pancake."

That pancake looked like it would sink to the bottom of her stomach like a rock. But she knew better than to refuse it. Picking up a fork, she cut off a bite-sized bit and popped it in her mouth.

"No syrup?"

"You know I don't like syrup, Mamm. But thank you for the breakfast." Dutifully, she ate another bite. It tasted like cardboard.

After refreshing Waneta's coffee, her mother sat down to watch her eat. "This is only my opinion, but I think you need to be more understanding of Mark's past."

"Mamm, I did everything I could. He's the one who is keeping me at an arm's length. He doesn't want to be close to me."

"Take another bite, child."

147

Feeling like she was growing younger by the second, Waneta did as she was bid. Chewing slowly, she watched the second hand on the clock above the sink make its way around the dial. She had about five more minutes, then she was going to be able to leave.

And what a blessed relief that would be!

After sneaking a piece of bacon off her plate and eating half of it, her father spoke. "Dear, do you remember when I told you that I didn't learn English until I was in seventh grade?"

She set down her fork. "*Jah*. You said it was difficult."

"It was harder than that. I went from only speaking Amish to having to learn to both speak and write English. I was frustrated with myself and more than a little resentful with my best friend, Arnie."

"Why was that?"

"Arnie's parents had taught him and his sister English on their own, years before. Arnie and Mercy sailed through all the lessons while I struggled."

Forgetting about the time, Waneta watched her father. He didn't often share stories about his past. Especially stories like this, about times that he had been struggling.

Leaning back, his eyes clouded. "I would mess up spelling simple words and struggled with having the most basic of conversations. Arnie and Mercy corrected and teased me. All the time. Other kids heard and decided to tease me, too.

"Here I was, thirteen. Strong, already used to hard work and a lot of responsibilities on the farm—but suddenly I was being made to feel stupid and weak." He shook his head. "I didn't like it."

Pushing the pancake away, Neeta rested her elbows on the table. "You weren't stupid, Daed. You just had to catch up."

"What I'm trying to tell ya is that my struggles almost ended my friendship with Arnie. He never did try to understand why I was struggling so much. Instead of helping me, he teased me about all my mistakes."

"I helped him, though," Mamm piped up.

"*Jah*, she did. That's one of the reasons I fell in love with her." While Mamm blushed like the schoolgirl she used to be, Daed looked a little sheepish. "Even after all this time, I guess I'm still a little upset about all that teasing."

At last, Waneta understood the point he'd been trying to make. "You think that I'm not being sympathetic enough about Mark's past."

"No one at his house taught him how to have good relationships, dear," Mamm said. "No one taught him how to love. Instead of growing up in a home where he felt safe and protected, he grew up with parents who treated him like a responsibility they never asked for."

"Then his mother took off," Daed added.

Mamm nodded. "Not long after, his brother left him, too."

"And then Mark was accused of that girl's assault and the whole community chose to believe the worst of him," Waneta said quietly.

"I'm sure he ain't an easy man to be around," her mother murmured. "But wouldn't you rather choose to think that he just needs someone to care enough about him to teach him about love and relationships?"

"You're making me feel awful."

"I don't want you to feel bad, child. But, well, maybe be more patient with him. He cares about you very much. I know he does."

Standing up, Neeta rinsed off her plate, then pulled out her cooler from the refrigerator. Once again, it was heavier than usual. There was obviously a lot of extra food in there. "How did you know I was sharing some of my food with Mark? Did he tell you?"

Joining her at the sink, her mother said, "I knew because I raised you, daughter. You would never let another person go hungry if you could help it."

Turning, she wrapped her arms around her mother's waist and hugged her tight. "*Danke*, Mamm. You are the best mother a girl could ever ask for. Daed, you are wonderful-*gut*, too."

While Daed laughed, her mother kissed her

brow. "You are a good girl. Now you'd best go or Henry ain't going to be happy." Looking at the clock, she said, "You're running a bit behind this morning, you know."

"*Jah*. You are going to have to pedal a little faster than normal to make up for your dawdling this morning," Daed said.

As Waneta walked out the door, tote bag in one hand, loaded cooler in the other, she had to laugh. Her parents were wonderful, that was true. But they definitely weren't perfect.

None of them were.

Yet another thing to remember.

She hurried down the road to Blooms and Berries, hoping Mr. Lehmann wasn't going to be too upset with her. Hopefully, Mark got there on time and took care of most of the usual morning chores.

The nursery was quiet when she opened the retail store's door. Both Mark and Mr. Lehmann were sipping coffee and talking quietly in front of the main counter. Henry looked a little listless while Mark's expression was shadowed.

This was mighty unusual. Most days when she arrived, Mr. Lehmann was already busy with some task and usually had a list of chores waiting for her the minute she arrived.

"Oh, here you are, Neeta," he said instead. "I guess it is just about that time to open."

A terrible sense of foreboding settled inside

her. What had happened now? She glanced Mark's way. Hopefully, he wasn't involved in another crisis.

"What's wrong?" she asked, hoping and praying that Mark was all right . . . and that he wasn't about to stonewall her again.

Mark and Mr. Lehmann shared a look. "Please, tell me," she pleaded.

"All right, then," Mr. Lehmann said as he stepped closer. After a slight pause, he blurted, "Amy Miller was attacked last night."

After dropping her things on the ground, she rushed toward him. Like most other Amish girls in the area, Neeta had known Amy for years. "What do you mean?"

"June found Amy injured in her front yard last night," Mark said when their boss looked like he couldn't get the words out. "Someone tried to rape her. When she fought back and screamed, he hit her several times. He knocked her out. She was unconscious when June came upon her."

Tears pricked her eyes. "Is . . . Is she okay now?"

Mr. Lehmann nodded. "From what I understand, she's shaken up and scared, but okay. As okay as she can be after such an ordeal." Looking at her sadly, he continued. "She's home and resting now."

"Thank goodness."

Mr. Lehmann nodded. "*Jah*. For sure. Her

beau, Abraham, is mighty upset, however. He's already been at the sheriff's office, demanding answers."

"Demanding answers? She doesn't know who did it?"

"*Nee.* It seems the man had a mask on his face. Of course, when she came to, he was nowhere to be found. June didn't see him, either," Mark supplied, his voice carefully flat.

Waneta shuddered. "I can't believe that this happened in our town. Ag—" She stopped herself from saying again.

"*Nee*, you can say it. It happened again." Mark's eyes looked so dark they were almost black. "I'm surprised you didn't hear about it on the way here."

"*Jah*, I thought maybe you had heard the news and decided to stay away," Mr. Lehmann blurted.

"I didn't hear anything. My mother made me pancakes and wanted to talk. Then, I was so worried about running late, I didn't talk to anyone the whole way here. How did you both hear about it?"

"I heard at the diner this morning," Mr. Lehmann said. "It's all anyone could talk about."

"Henry told me as soon as I got here," Mark added quietly. His tone was stiff and awkward sounding.

Usually, Waneta would have asked Mr. Lehmann if she could leave and go right to see Amy. But the pain in Mark's eyes was so fresh, she didn't have the heart to leave him. Amy had a lot of people who would be surrounding her with concern and love.

But Mark? He only had Mr. Lehmann and her.

"I'll be sure to stop by Amy's house tonight," she said, taking care to keep her voice light.

"You sure you're okay with waiting so long?" Mr. Lehmann asked. "If you don't feel like working, I understand."

"I'm sure. I think I need to work." Eager to change the topic, she said, "Mark, did you get the cashbox ready or turn on the solar fans?"

After visibly gathering himself together, he shook his head. "*Nee*, but I'll go do that right now."

"I'll work on the cashbox, then," she said, just as two cars pulled into the parking lot.

She needed to take her mother's advice to heart and imagine what it was like for Mark. He was expecting the worst from her. That was what his wary, blank look was all about.

It looked like she was going to have to start making sure that she surprised him with how different she could be.

Chapter 15

Wednesday, August 10

Mark felt like he was in the middle of a recurring nightmare. From the moment Henry had told him about Amy Miller's attack, he'd been in a daze. His thoughts were hazy. Scattered.

The firm hold he usually had on his emotions felt tenuous. Worse, he felt like he was on the verge of losing everything good that he'd found since his return. That was difficult to swallow. Were all of his recent blessings truly that fragile? He hated the idea that everything he was so hopeful about could vanish in an instant, before he'd even gotten used to them.

He felt paranoid, too. The timing of Amy's attack seemed too coincidental. He couldn't shake the idea that it had something to do with him, like someone had used his return as an excuse to hurt an innocent woman.

Just as quickly, shame consumed him. How could he even be fixating on how this event affected him and his life? An innocent girl had almost gotten raped, and he was upset with how the community was going to perceive *him*. When was he ever going to be able to shed his past and not view everything from a tainted perspective?

For most of the morning, Waneta worked in relative silence by his side. She darted wary glances his way in between customers, most of whom were Amish and seemed to be trying their best to ignore Mark. Though she wasn't acting completely distant, she did seem to be acting a little quieter around him.

He was relieved when Henry eventually asked him to work on one of the flower beds in front of the store. Henry liked to have the beds filled with seasonal annuals and switched them out a couple of times a year.

As he dug holes and added a row of yellow chrysanthemums, Mark turned his thoughts back to Waneta.

He wished they were someplace more private. Then he could ask her why she seemed so distant. He needed to know what was behind her silence.

Was she acting reserved because he'd been so aloof all week? Or was it something darker? Maybe she was afraid of him again. Maybe she was afraid of whoever had attacked Amy. Maybe she was simply upset about what had happened. Any of those options seemed like a good possibility.

If they were, he wanted to be there for her.

Comfort her as best he could. He cared about her, as much as he cared about Henry.

"Excuse me?" a woman in running shorts and tank top called out from the door. "Could you help me with these begonias? I just bought four pallets and I need some help getting them to my Jeep."

"Of course." Jumping to his feet, he brushed off his hands, then turned to the laden cart. When she pointed to where her vehicle was, at the bottom of a sloping hill, he realized it would be easiest to simply carry each pallet there. "Lead the way and I'll follow," he said as he picked up a tray.

"Thank you so much." When they started walking to her car, she chatted excitedly about her gardening plans.

Back and forth they went, Mark silently carrying flowers and bags of potting soil while the woman talked about her yard, the barbecue they were about to host, and her hope that the deer wouldn't eat everything before the party.

"What do you think?" she asked when they were making the final trek to her SUV.

"I couldn't say," he murmured as he placed her last two bags of mulch on the floor of her backseat. "Deer do pretty much whatever they like. Ain't so?"

When he turned to smile at her, she pressed her hand to her lips. "I'm so sorry. I've been rattling on about flower beds and parties like you are interested."

"I don't mind you telling me about your plans at all." Actually, as far as he was concerned, the lady could talk about barbecues and begonias all day long. The easy conversation had been a nice break from the worries of the day.

And sure enough, when he went back to finish the bed he'd been working on, his thoughts returned to Amy and Waneta.

At two o'clock that afternoon, Mark was back inside the store and they finally had a break from the steady stream of customers.

Since Henry was in his office, Mark decided it was the perfect time to finally break the ice. But just as he was attempting to figure out the best way to bring up the subject, Waneta placed one cool hand on his bare forearm.

He looked at her in surprise.

"Sorry if I startled you. I just . . . well, I wondered, now that a couple of hours have passed, how you were coping with the news?"

Her touch, combined with her concern for him, was a soothing balm. An unexpected one. "I don't know. My mind is kind of a muddle right now."

"I feel the same way. The whole thing is just so horrible. I'm so worried about Amy." She rubbed her hands over her arms. "Who do you think would have done such a terrible thing?"

"I couldn't begin to guess. I only know it wasn't me."

"Of course it wasn't."

She sounded so sure. So resolute. Relief filled him. "You really believe that, don't you?"

"*Jah*. Don't you want me to believe that?"

"Of course I do. I just thought, you know, with my history and all . . ."

"Your history has nothing to do with what happened to Amy."

Though he was still concerned that Amy's attack actually did have something to do with him, he nodded.

Looking pleased that he was listening to her, Waneta continued. "As a matter of fact, Mark, I think you need to learn that there are some people in the world who only want the best for you."

"Is that right?"

"Absolutely."

And is one of those people you? He ached to ask that.

But how could he? It sounded like he was fishing for compliments. Or maybe it just made him seem really desperate. He changed the topic. "Did you ride your bike or walk today?"

"I was going to ride, but I got such a late start, I decided to walk instead. The later I leave, the more traffic is on the roads."

"Okay. I am going to walk you home

tonight. I'll come get you tomorrow morning, too."

"Mark, that ain't necessary."

"It is. If some man attacked your friend in her yard, then you certainly aren't safe walking by yourself."

Her expression softened. "All right, then. You're right. I will feel safer."

Mark sighed. He was glad she wasn't arguing about her safety. "Since it's so quiet now, why don't you go eat?"

"Don't you want to eat together?"

"Henry didn't offer that today, Waneta. And I don't want to ask him, either. He's just as rattled about Amy as we are."

"Oh. Well, just to let you know, I brought you some leftovers. Rather, my *mamm* packed you some."

"Maybe you could leave them for me?" he asked gently. "I'll fish them out when it's my turn."

She nodded, then after making him promise to call if he needed help, she walked into the storage room.

Unable to help himself, he smiled. Maybe everything was going to be all right between them. She seemed to trust him again, and he was grateful for that.

Now he needed to make Waneta realize that he was someone she could depend on.

Maybe he could start walking her to and from

work. It was a little old-fashioned, but he'd have the opportunity to have her to himself twice a day. There was a benefit to that.

Jah. Maybe he could start taking her to supper sometimes after work, too. Or they could set a date to get that dog. Then they'd have lots of reasons to see each other outside of work.

The door chimed.

Mark turned to greet the newcomer. "Afternoon. Welcome to Blooms and Berries. We've got plenty of—" He stopped abruptly as every muscle in his body tensed up. "Calvin."

His brother stepped closer. He was wearing dark jeans, a rust-colored T-shirt that had obviously seen better days, and a smirk. "Oh, so you do know me. I wasn't sure."

The comment stung, but he figured it was justified. Mark definitely had ignored Calvin when he was lurking in Waneta's yard.

However, his brother could have handled things differently. He should have been more open. Calvin could have stopped by the house any evening to talk to him since he'd returned. Instead, he'd been hanging out with Lora and avoiding the sheriff.

Now, here he was, coming to see him in the middle of a workday. Where Waneta would see him.

Mark wasn't ready for that. Calvin could ruin everything between himself and Waneta.

"What are you doing here?"

Calvin glared. "That's all you have to say?"

"No, but that's all I intend to say here. This ain't the place to have our reunion."

Looking around the large shop, he shrugged. "It looks good enough to me."

"Well, it ain't. This is Mr. Lehmann's place."

"You and Mr. Lehmann. Always so close. You'd think he was your flesh and blood."

Mark had spent many hours wishing Henry was just that. And because of his regard for him, Mark wasn't about to do anything to jeopardize Henry's trust.

Especially not talking with a brother who seemed to be itching for a fight.

Walking around the counter, Mark said, "Calvin, I do want to see you. I really do want to catch up. Why don't you come to the house after I get home from work? I'll be home by six or seven."

"That's all you've got to say?"

"For now? *Jah*."

Uncertainty flickered in his eyes before he glared. "You know, when we were growing up, I always thought you tried too hard to be something you weren't. Looks like that habit has only gotten worse."

It looked like they were going to have to talk right there anyway. "I did my best to look after you," Mark said. "You know I did."

162

"If you had really cared about me, you would have left, too."

"Someone had to look out for Daed. Look out for our home."

Calvin grunted. "Because Daed treated us so well and our house was such a great place."

"It was what we had." It was also more than he'd managed to obtain on his own. "Do you have better?"

For the first time, a hint of vulnerability clouded Calvin's features. "Not yet."

Another time, in another situation, Mark would have loved that answer. It would have signified that all the things he'd wanted his little brother to have had come to fruition.

But now, seeing him angry and agitated— almost looking for a fight?—he only felt wary and disappointed.

"I need to talk to you about the house."

"What about it?" Mark asked.

"It's half mine. The money we could get for it would be half mine, too."

It took everything Mark had not to show how disappointed he was. Calvin had sought him out for money. That was at the heart of their reunion. But even though he knew that, he couldn't push him away.

Feeling weary and far older than his years, Mark said, "Come over tonight and we'll talk. We can have supper together."

163

"Do you cook now?"

"I can grill a steak and put some corn and potatoes in the oven."

Just as Calvin looked about to answer him, Waneta and Henry came into the store. Each was looking at Calvin intently. Henry was obviously assessing him, taking in his T-shirt, jeans, and heavy-soled black leather boots.

Waneta was simply staring at him curiously.

Mark knew he needed to say something. But while he debated how to best handle the introductions, Waneta stepped forward.

"Calvin? You're back!" Her smile was tremulous.

For the first time since he'd walked in the door, his brother looked unsure of himself. If he wasn't so worried about what Calvin was going to say, he would have smiled. Waneta had that effect on a person.

"I'm surprised you remember me," he said.

She looked confused. "Why?"

"I left a long time ago."

"That's true. And you're obviously English now."

"I got rid of my suspenders the moment I got on the bus."

"Ah." Waneta looked more hesitant. Even a little nervous. Mark knew she wasn't taken aback by someone deciding not to join the faith. It certainly happened from time to time.

No, she was wary because of his tone of voice. Calvin sounded snarky and belligerent.

"Like I said before, brother," Mark said. "I'll see you this evening. After I get home from work."

Calvin folded his arms over his chest. "I may not have time then."

Feeling deflated, he nodded. "Whenever you do have time to see me, I'll be there waiting."

"Still waiting, aren't you? Still waiting for someone to see the good in ya."

"He ain't waiting for that, boy," Henry said as he strode forward. "Your brother is a good man and always has been. But it is time you left. Unless you came in to shop, of course."

"I ain't shopping here."

"Then we got nothing to say to each other. Do we?" Henry said.

Waneta looked even more nervous. Her eyes kept darting from Calvin to Mark to Henry.

Mark walked to the door and opened it. "Come by the house later," he said again.

Two cars pulled into the parking lot. Soon they were going to have an audience. Mark feared that would spur Calvin's anger on.

As he walked to the door, Calvin glanced at Mark. "She's better-looking up close, Mark," he said loud enough for Waneta to hear. "No wonder you were panting after her the other day."

Mark's hand clenched. Really, it was all he could do not to shove him out the door.

Obviously glad to have gotten that reaction, Calvin laughed before turning, and kept walking as two customers entered the shop.

"May I help ya?" Waneta asked.

"We're interested in flowering trees."

Looking pleased to escape the tension in the room, Waneta walked them over to one of the greenhouses. The man who had just come in simply wanted to look around.

"What was that about?" Henry asked when they were standing alone again.

"I'm not sure."

"Did you know he was back?"

Mark nodded. Oh, yes, he'd known. He'd fooled himself into thinking it had been a secret he could keep a little longer, too.

It was now obvious that he couldn't have been more wrong. Calvin had returned for a reason and Mark feared that it had something to do with him, his anger, and maybe even Amy Miller.

Chapter 16

Even at twenty-four years of age, rejection still hurt. As Calvin walked to the far corner of the parking lot where he'd parked his bike, he wondered what he had expected would happen. Had he really thought that Mark was going to drop everything, give him a hug, and announce that he was glad to see him?

Maybe.

He would have never admitted it out loud, but even after Mark had ignored him standing in the Cains' yard, Calvin still hoped that their next reunion would be different.

That's what love was. Well, what it was supposed to be, anyway. An emotion that overruled bruised feelings and past mistakes. Something so strong that it couldn't be taken away.

He'd been wrong.

He'd needed Mark's help, too. Things were getting worse with the gang he owed money to. They'd told him from the beginning that they didn't forget about debts that were owed.

Now he owed almost as much in interest as the original amount he'd borrowed. He was in over his head. He was going to have to find some way to convince Mark to sell the house and give him half the money.

If that didn't work, Calvin was going to have to go another route. Think about using a bit of coercion. Maybe Mark could be convinced to pay him off so Calvin wouldn't disturb his new, little perfect life and sweet romance with Waneta Cain.

Weighing his options, he decided to head over to Munfordville. There were a couple of places there to eat that offered decent food for cheap.

Just as he pulled his key from his jeans pocket, a sheriff pulled up next to him.

For a split second, Calvin considered starting up his bike and running, but it was doubtful he'd make it far. Most likely all it would do was make things worse.

Therefore, he stayed put and stared at the sheriff, his expression carefully blank.

"You Calvin Fisher?" the sheriff said as he got out of his vehicle. He was both walking and talking slowly, like he feared Calvin was going to pull a gun out and start shooting.

"Yeah."

"I'm Sheriff Brewer. I have some things I need to talk about with you. Let's go down to the station. There's a place to talk there in private."

No way was he going to go to a sheriff's station if he could help it. "We can't discuss whatever it is right now?"

"In the Blooms and Berries parking lot? No."

"I'm kind of busy right now. I ain't in the mood to get questioned, especially since I didn't do anything wrong."

Sheriff Brewer narrowed his eyes. "I didn't say you did. You're not in trouble. But we do need to chat. It won't take long."

Calvin inserted the key into his cycle's ignition. "If I'm not in trouble, then I don't have to chat with anyone."

"I'd hate to force you to come with me." His voice had turned hard.

"And I'd hate to contact my lawyer. But I will if need be."

"You have a lawyer?"

He didn't. But he hated how the sheriff thought he wasn't good enough to get one. "Yeah. So, I'll be seeing you around." Facing his bike now, he exhaled. He'd done good. He'd held his ground but didn't lose his temper or make things worse.

Just as he climbed on and was about to punch the ignition, the sheriff spoke again. "I know you brought some drugs to Lora Weaver's. I know you hit her."

Though he knew he shouldn't take the bait, he said, "Did she press charges against me?"

"No, but she could have. You bruised her face pretty good. She could have been seriously hurt."

"If she didn't press charges, she ain't my problem."

"So you aren't denying any of my accusations?"

"No. I'm saying that I have nothing to say about anything."

"Lora told us that you have access to heavy drugs."

Why had she told them that? With effort, he choked back a laugh. "That's rich."

"Why do you say that?"

"I'm not saying I was there or that I know anything about drugs. But, come on. Lora don't need anyone to give her drugs. She can get them just fine on her own."

"You sound like you know a lot about her."

"I know that she's a sad sort of person with time on her hands. I know that whatever she's up to ain't my problem."

Sheriff Brewer nodded slowly. Then, just when Calvin was sure he was going to leave, he blurted, "What about Amy Miller, then?"

"Who's that?"

"Her name doesn't ring a bell?"

"Obviously not." Calvin didn't trust the way the sheriff's eyes brightened. "Who is she?"

"Oh, she's just an Amish girl who was assaulted last night. The man who attacked her was wearing a mask, so she can't identify him. We're going to have to rely on DNA."

Calvin knew his heart was starting to race. That was the real reason that the sheriff had been watching for him. It didn't have anything to do with Lora or a Baggie of pot. It was about the girl.

And DNA? What did that mean? Had Brewer planned on taking him in and swabbing his mouth or something? "That's real sad," he finally bit out. "But that girl don't have anything to do with me."

"Maybe. Maybe not. Calvin, I want to know what you were doing last night."

"I was in Munfordville."

"Any specific place?"

"Yeah. I was sitting on my bed, watching television in my motel room."

"And the name of this motel is . . . ?"

Calvin couldn't remember. It was just another run-down dive offering rooms for thirty-six dollars a night. "I don't remember the name exactly. Cave something. Or maybe it was Hart Hotel?"

"You don't recall?" Skepticism was thick in his tone.

"No, but it ain't like there are lots of places to choose from. Go ask around if you want."

Sheriff Brewer looked ticked. "I'll be doing that."

It was happening. He was going to get attempted rape or assault, or something, pinned on him. Just because he was a Fisher.

Or maybe Lora had been talking bad about him. Or Mark had.

That idea hurt like crazy but seemed possible. As the bitterness coated his insides, he lifted his chin. "Don't want to tell you how to do your job or nothing, but it sure sounds like you picked the wrong brother to question."

Sheriff Brewer straightened his shoulders. "Care to explain that?"

"What do I need to explain? Weren't you the cop who arrested Mark two years ago?"

"It was me. But I didn't arrest him. Only brought him in for questioning."

"Well, I could be wrong, but I heard that men don't change their habits about things like that. He could have returned and gotten back to his old ways."

Looking like he was smelling something rotten, Brewer said, "Now I've heard everything. A man turning on his own brother."

"If that's the worst thing you've ever heard, you should have stopped by our house growing up. You'd have learned then that nothing is off limits. Not for brothers, and not how parents can treat their sons. But, oh yeah, no one cared about us then. You only care about the Fisher boys when you need to pin a crime on somebody." While those words hung in the air, he let the engine roar to life.

As bitterness and regret filled his lungs, he roared out of the parking lot, practically daring the sheriff to follow him or give him a ticket for speeding.

But as he sped down the highway, no one was following him. Not the sheriff. Not his brother. Just his memories of the things that had happened in his house.

Turned out that he didn't need anything more to spur him on. He decided to ride until he got his emotions under control, and then head back to town.

There was something he needed to do. Something that couldn't be helped.

Chapter 17

Waneta had been thankful that Mr. and Mrs. Johnson were so interested in organic produce. Standing in the vegetable greenhouse, surrounded by the scent of fresh herbs and row after row of peppers and tomatoes, she'd answered all of the couple's questions about growing tomatoes of their own.

After they purchased four plants and a green plastic watering can, she'd met Mark at the counter. He still looked upset.

For a moment, she considered not even mentioning Calvin's surprise visit, but she decided that would be wrong. Surely, it was better to identify the elephant in the room instead of pretending that it didn't exist?

"I didn't know your brother was back," she finally said, keeping it simple.

"Yeah. He arrived a couple of days ago."

His voice was flat, and Waneta was pretty sure that the muscles in his neck had tightened. Every response that came to her mind sounded too trite.

Keep it simple.

She had almost elected to keep silent. But when she noticed just how upset he was—his dark eyes almost black, so filled with pain—she decided to say something. Even if it wasn't the right thing to say.

"He looks different than I remember."

A bark of laughter erupted from Mark. The opposite of joyful. It sounded dark and bitter. Frustrated.

"*Jah*. He surely does."

"I had heard he'd become everything English. I guess that rumor was true."

"I knew he would," he said slowly. "He . . . Well, it seemed he was never suited to our way of life. Never content. Always hoping for something different. Better."

Finally, he was opening up! Maybe he was realizing that he could trust her. Feeling hopeful, she said, "He found it, then. That's a good thing, right?"

"*Nee*. What he chose ain't better. It ain't anything close to that."

She'd been wrong, then. "I'm sorry. Obviously, I'm struggling with finding the right words to say."

He pressed a hand to his face. "*Nee*," he said softly. "Don't apologize. You haven't done anything wrong. I'm the one who is sorry. Seeing him upsets me. Seeing him around you upsets me even more. I never know how he's going to act. I never know what he's going to say or do. I'm afraid he's going to offend you or hurt your feelings." Looking down at his feet, he said, "Maybe even something worse. I don't know how to handle it."

She had no idea what he was referring to, but she couldn't imagine that his brother could ever affect her that much. She wasn't a weak girl.

It was time he realized that. "You don't need to worry about me, Mark."

He paused, then said, "*Nee*, I do. He's erratic. He's saying and doing things that I don't understand." Rubbing a hand across his face, he added, "It makes me crazy." Looking around the empty space, with all the stock perfectly organized, he added, "You may not know this, but I like things in proper order. It sets my mind at ease."

"I actually have noticed that about you," she teased. "After all, you are the one who rearranged these shelves."

"I think it's a consequence of how we were brought up. Growing up, my parents never did what was expected of them. It made me want to be around people and things I can count on. But that's not really possible."

"Which is hard on you," she said, understanding him even better now.

He nodded. "Waneta, all that has been going through my head. Well, all that, and Amy getting hurt and Calvin returning. It's set me off. I know it's confused you, too. I'm sorry for the way I've been acting this week."

"You have been running a bit hot and cold."

"I have been. I'm a grown man, but I don't know how to protect myself from giving into these mood swings." After a pause, he added more quietly, "Or how to protect you from harm, period."

"You need to stop worrying about me so much. It's just me. Waneta."

"You are just you. But, don't you see? That means something. You mean something to me."

She didn't know whether to give him a hug or burst into tears. His words were heartfelt. So sweet.

Looking embarrassed, he said, "I guess it's pretty obvious that I like you. I want to get to know you better and I want you to get to know me better, too. But as hard as I try, it seems that I can't separate my past from the present. It taints everything I'm trying to do. I feel like I'm living in fear of you finding one more thing that will be the final straw. That will make you finally turn away from me."

His honest words made her pulse flutter. Again, she felt helpless by her naiveté. She wished she had more experience in relationships.

Since she didn't, she could only rely on honesty and hope it was enough for him. "I want to get to know you better, too, Mark. I don't know what secrets you're hiding, but I don't plan to judge you on either your past or your brother."

"You sure about that?"

She shrugged. She didn't feel sure about anything. Not his past, not her feelings, not even his scary brother. "Does it matter?" she asked. "Do we have to know everything about each other in order to have a friendship? Or to even have something more than that?"

He shook his head slowly. "*Nee*. But will you promise me something? If you do start feeling like you need more space from me, if you feel like whatever is happening between us isn't making you happy, tell me, okay?"

"Okay. I can do that."

His expression warmed, though she felt a new tension brewing between them.

"May I come over tonight?"

"You may, but why? Do you need something?"

Looking a little embarrassed, he said, "I want to call on you properly, like your parents would expect a suitor to act."

Knowing that he was right, that her parents would need to see him do everything that they expected, even if it was all slightly old-fashioned, given their situation, she nodded.

"Maybe they'll even let me take you out for an evening stroll. We can look at the fireflies."

"Maybe they will." She smiled, liking that idea.

Mark smiled, too. For once, his happiness even

reached his eyes. "I better get to work, then. We'll talk later," he said before turning away.

She watched him stride over to Mr. Lehmann, chat with him for a moment, then exit out the back door toward the far greenhouses.

Watching him made her feel a little mushy inside. A little optimistic about their future.

It also made her wonder if everything between them was on the verge of falling apart . . . even if it had never really had a chance to begin yet.

"Waneta, we are so glad to see you," Mrs. Miller said as she let her into their house. "I guess you heard about Amy?"

"First thing today. I'm sorry I didn't get here earlier. I had to work."

"We've had our share of visitors today. Poor Amy was so exhausted by the time the last group of young people left."

"Oh? Would you like me to come back tomorrow?"

"Of course not. You and Amy have been close for years." Her lips pursed. "Unfortunately, some of the men and women who stopped by only came over to get information. My Francis put a stop to that."

"I bet he did." Mr. Miller was stocky and had worked for many years up in the Michigan logging camps. He was big and burly and had no patience for people who didn't adhere to his standards.

"Amy just woke up from a nap. Her father has been sitting by her bed, watching her sleep."

"I'm sure he's been a great source of comfort."

"He has, but you can give him a break. Come along now." Two steps away from her daughter's door, she turned to face Waneta again. "You might want to prepare yourself, dear. Amy was pretty beaten up," she said just as she opened the door and led the way inside.

The moment Waneta saw Amy's bruised and battered face and arms, she wished she would have taken that advice to heart.

Amy wasn't just a little bruised. She looked like her attacker had slammed her face on the pavement. Cuts and stitches were on her cheek and above her eye. Her nose was swollen and her eyes were blackened.

Even more disturbing were the dark fingertip bruises around her throat and on her collarbone. Someone had gripped her hard. Really hard.

"Neeta," she said. "You came to see me."

Her voice was hoarse and rough sounding. And the expression in her eyes! She looked so sad.

Tears pricked Waneta's eyes as she darted forward. "Oh, Amy. I am so sorry."

"Me, too." Her bottom lip trembled before she glanced at her father. "But I'll be all right. God was with me today. That is why I wasn't hurt worse."

Standing up, Mr. Miller nodded. "What she

says is true. Though she was hurt badly, the Lord helped her through it. The nurse said she's going to heal and be just fine. That was a blessing."

Waneta had a strong faith, but she wasn't sure how it was possible to look at anything that had happened as a blessing. Feeling at a loss for words, she simply smiled as Mr. Miller told Amy that he'd give the two of them some privacy for a half hour.

When the door closed behind him, Amy exhaled. "You had perfect timing, Waneta. I love my father dearly, but I needed a break from his hovering."

"I'm glad I came at this time of day, then. You are making me feel useful."

Shifting against her pillow, Amy tried to smile. "Glad I could help."

"I sure am sorry you were attacked. I bet it was scary."

"It was horrible. I'm still shaken up. I don't know how I'm ever going to be able to walk anywhere alone again."

"I bet you won't have to. Your parents and Abraham will no doubt keep a close eye on you for months."

"I think you are right. Abraham was so upset. When he first saw me, he looked like he couldn't decide whether to hold me close or go after Mark Fisher."

She was stunned. "Why would he want to go after Mark?"

Amy looked at her strangely. "Come on. You know why."

"*Nee*. I really don't. I heard you didn't see who attacked you." All at once, a horrible thought came to her. "Wait a minute. Was that not true?"

"*Nee*, it was true. The man had a mask on and I didn't recognize his voice," she said weakly. "But we all know that Mark hurt Bethany. So I'm thinking that it must have been Mark who hurt me."

"He didn't!"

Amy stared at her. "If not him, who else could it be?"

Feeling like she was destined to continually stand up for Mark, who had done nothing to deserve such harsh treatment, Waneta said, "I have no idea, but I know it wasn't Mark. He didn't hurt Bethany, Amy. He was taken in for questioning and then released. Sheriff Brewer cleared his name."

"Well, it was someone I knew. I do know that much."

"How? What did he say?"

After glancing at the door to make sure it was shut, Amy whispered, "He yelled at me when he had me down on the ground. He said that he knew I dressed up and went to the mall and the movies with Abraham last weekend."

Waneta was surprised. Belatedly, she recalled that Abraham's parents hadn't minded him parking his truck in their field and that he and Amy hadn't been baptized yet. Technically, they were still in their *rumspringa.* "I had forgotten that you both still went out and did things like that."

Amy looked at her sharply. "'Like that'?" she repeated sharply. "You make it sound like we are doing something wrong."

"I didn't mean to make it sound that way," she said quickly. "I meant only that I'd forgotten that you still hadn't joined the faith."

"Still? Boy, now, that sounds judgmental."

"I'm not judging you." At least, she was trying not to.

"I hope not. Because there's nothing wrong with still going out and experimenting with English ways. Abraham said we have time before we have to join the church."

"*Jah.* Of course." Feeling more uncomfortable, Waneta said, "Maybe the man who attacked you was English. He could have seen you at the movies and followed you home so he'd know where you lived or something."

"Maybe, but I doubt it."

"What did Sheriff Brewer think?"

"He isn't sure who it could be. But then, I didn't tell him about what the man said."

"Why not?" It was hard not to raise her voice. "It sounds important."

183

"Waneta, he might have told my parents!"

"They don't know that you've been going to the mall and movies?" Waneta was incredulous. Surely, neither Amy nor her parents were that naïve?

"Of course they don't know."

"But they know you and Abraham are still doing things like tha . . . Right?"

Amy sighed. "*Nee*. They don't." Impatiently, she brushed a stray strand of hair away from her face. "Waneta, I don't know why we're even talking about this. What matters is that Mark Fisher is hurting people again."

Waneta stepped away. She felt like she was in an impossible situation, but she also knew that she had to do what was right. What was in her heart. "Amy, I feel sorry for you and I would have never wanted you to get attacked like you did. I will pray for your recovery. But I am friends with Mark now. I can't allow you to blame him for something I know he didn't do."

"Do you really *know* he didn't do it?"

"Of course."

"And how do you know he is so innocent, Neeta? Were you with him last night? Are you his alibi?"

She was tempted to say she was. Tempted to lie. But that lie could only blow up in her face. "I wasn't. But I talked to him about it this morning. He was really upset and shocked. Just like I was."

Amy looked at her curiously before understanding dawned. "You two are working together at the nursery, aren't ya?"

"*Jah.*"

"Then I'll tell you the same thing you just told me, Neeta. I am sorry for you. I hope this never happens to you. But if you continue to hang around him, chances are good that something will happen to you, too." Lifting her chin, she said, "I think I need to rest now. Can you see yourself out?"

"Amy, please don't be mad. You know I'm only trying to stand up for a friend."

"I thought *I* was your friend."

Since it was now obvious that Amy wasn't going to try to understand her point of view, Waneta started for the door. "I'm leaving now, but I really do think you are making a mistake about not telling the truth to Sheriff Brewer. You shouldn't lie about what that man said."

"You sound so holier than thou. I can't wait for the day when you realize that it was a mistake to be so judgmental."

Even bruised, Amy had an answer for everything. Feeling hopeless about the situation, she walked right from Amy's room to the front door and quietly let herself out.

She felt a little guilty. The right thing to do would have been to inform Mr. and Mrs. Miller that she was leaving, but she couldn't find the nerve to do it. She was too upset and distressed about everything Amy had said.

Walking back home, Waneta felt so isolated. For years now, she'd gone to work and gone home. Sure, she'd enjoyed many friends in the area, but she hadn't made time to do things with them in a very long time. Instead, she'd found her happiness with her parents and in her work at the nursery.

Perhaps that's why Amy's comments had stung so badly. Not only did Amy seem more than a little derisive about Waneta's choices, it seemed like she faulted Waneta for staying on the straight and narrow.

As she walked along, feeling the heat of the late-afternoon sun warm her shoulders and smelling the faint scent of honeysuckle in the air, she realized that she couldn't see anyone for miles.

The chill that ran down her spine caught her by surprise.

She realized that if someone did come out of nowhere and attacked her, no one would hear her scream. She'd have to fight him off on her own.

As she turned the corner and saw her house and her two neighbors' houses in the distance, she breathed a sigh of relief. She was safe, for now.

But her pulse was racing so fast, she was starting to feel like she soon wasn't going to be safe.

Chapter 18

Wednesday evening, August 10

Someone had been in his house again. There was nothing blatant, just a couple of signs that stood out to him. A closet door left open that he knew he'd shut. Drops of water dotting the old stainless steel sink in the kitchen.

A bottle of Gatorade was missing from his refrigerator.

Mark wondered if his culprit had been Calvin or if there was another person in Horse Cave who was anxious to uncover all his secrets.

He wouldn't have been surprised if there was. He doubted it was Sheriff Brewer, but there were likely other people who were suspicious of him.

Maybe even someone like James Eicher, who'd acted so angry when he'd spotted him at Blooms and Berries on his first day at work.

He wasn't sure what the intruder had been looking for, however. He didn't have anything worth stealing and the house was so run-down that anything that was removed could be considered a blessing.

Ever since Mark had gotten home two hours

ago, he'd been pondering the possibilities over and over. It was a futile exercise for the most part, however. There were too many people he didn't trust, and they no doubt felt the same way about him.

Bending down, he picked up another armful of worn and dilapidated linoleum that he'd pulled off the kitchen floor. At last, it was all removed. After he sanded and stained the wood floor, it was going to look terrific. Knowing he was responsible for the transformation would feel good, too.

Pushing open the back door with his shoulder, he carefully navigated the two steps down to the cement pad leading to the old garage, and at last dropped the offending materials in the pile.

His shirt was soaked with sweat. Was the temperature ever going to cool off? Stretching his arms, he bent from one side to the other. He needed the moment to relax before he went inside to shower, grab something to eat, then mentally prepare himself to return to the Cains' house.

Rolling his shoulders, he exhaled, attempting to ease the knots that had formed there as he thought about Waneta and the way she made him smile.

He wasn't sure exactly how to be the type of suitor Waneta needed, but he was certainly going to give it a try. He would do just about anything in order to make her happy.

"Hey, Mark!" Lora Weaver called out from the top of his driveway.

Turning to her, Mark tried to summon some kind of welcoming expression. He wasn't sure why she'd come over, though. They'd been friends when they were young, but it had been more out of necessity than a real liking for each other. Now it seemed like they were polar opposites.

"Hey, Lora," he said at last.

As he imagined her reasons for stopping over, the only one that made sense was his brother. And that made him stop. He needed to say something about Calvin hurting her. "I'm glad you stopped by. I wanted to talk to you about Calvin, and see how you were feeling."

She interrupted him. "What's this you're doing?"

Feeling confused, but willing to let her lead the conversation, he pointed to the pile of old flooring. "Working on the house. Pulling off old linoleum. It's a miserable job."

"I bet. What was underneath it? Concrete?" she asked as she walked closer.

Glancing at her face, he noticed that her eyes were red and there were faint lines of strain around them. Maybe the sheriff had been wrong. Maybe she'd been hurt worse than anyone realized.

But since her expression was so pinched,

so earnest, he bided his time and continued talking about the house. "Actually, I found wood floors underneath. Oak in good condition, too." Unable to help himself, he rolled his eyes. "Only my parents would have placed linoleum over perfectly good hardwood."

She smiled tightly. "At least they cared about the place at one time, right?"

She had a point. "Yeah."

Reaching out, she fingered a yellowed, curled corner of linoleum. "Now that all this ugly flooring is out, I bet your place is going to look a lot better."

"Hope so."

"Of course it will. I mean, it couldn't have looked much worse," she joked.

Maybe it was because he was still stewing on the fact that someone had been inside, but her comment struck him as odd. "How do you know that?"

She looked at him curiously. "No reason. I mean, it's true, right?"

"It is true. But I'm wondering why you'd say such a thing. It ain't like you've been in here in years. Or have you?"

"Of course I haven't." Sounding hurt, she continued. "Why are you looking at me like I'm the one who put in all that ugly linoleum? I'm only making conversation."

"Someone came in my house today without my

knowledge. I'm trying to figure out who would do such a thing."

"Well, it sure wasn't me." She rubbed her palms on the tops of her thighs. Today she was wearing a long beige cotton skirt, white T-shirt, and flip-flops. It was close to being what any girl of their acquaintance who was dressed conservatively would usually wear. It was far different than the tank top and tight-fitting jeans she'd been wearing the first time they'd talked.

He wondered if it was a coincidence, or if she'd dressed like that purposely in order to remind him of their past.

Just as quickly, he disregarded that idea. He really was becoming paranoid. He needed to get a grip on himself. But first he needed to bring up the subject she seemed intent to avoid. "Lora, I wanted to tell you that I'm really sorry that Calvin hurt you."

"You know it was Calvin?"

"*Jah*. Sheriff Brewer told me. He said that Calvin was partying over at your house a couple of nights ago."

"Partying is a strange word to describe it, considering that he hit me."

Mark flinched. He was not his brother's keeper, but even now old habits seemed hard to shake. "I really am sorry. I hope you are healing?"

"Yeah. It's all right." She tilted her chin toward

the fading sunlight. "I'm still bruised, but the swelling's gone down."

Looking at the lingering discoloration on her cheek and around her eye, he felt even worse. "I really am sorry. I can't believe Calvin would hit a woman."

"It surprised me, too. But then, a lot of surprising things are happening around here these days."

"Like what?"

"Like me coming back last year. Like Calvin showing up. Like you courting Waneta Cain."

He didn't like the new, cool inflection in her voice. "I'm not going to talk about her with you."

"Why not?"

"You and Waneta are too different. You have nothing in common."

"Maybe she and I aren't all that different, Mark."

Waneta was sheltered, positive, and honest. At the moment, she seemed like the complete opposite of Lora Weaver, with her tainted past and hard edges. "I'm sorry, but I don't agree. Maybe one time you were alike, but you are very different now."

"You mean I'm very different than the girl I was." When he nodded, she lifted her chin. "Maybe you are very different than who you used to be, too, Mark. And maybe, just maybe, Calvin and you are a little like me and Waneta. Different on the outside but not so different in your heart."

Mark didn't know how to respond to that. Everything inside of him was wanting to refute her words, to tell her that she was wrong.

She sighed. "Calvin ain't here, is he?"

"*Nee*. I don't know where he is."

She looked puzzled. "Oh. I thought he was going to see you today."

"He did. But he stopped by to see me at work. I told him I didn't want to talk to him there. I told him to stop by tonight."

"Oh. Do you think he'll stop over?"

"I doubt it. He wasn't happy with me. He raced off on his motorcycle with a giant chip on his shoulder."

Lora gazed at him sadly. "He's kind of a lost soul right now."

Though he was more than ready to say something scathing, he knew she was giving him the opening that he desperately needed to learn more about his brother. "How can you say something like that, Lora? He hit you."

"Yeah, he did. I've forgiven him, though. I know he probably feels bad about it. I think he's in a world of trouble."

"I'm pretty sure that is the case. He always was a champion of making bad decisions."

"Maybe so, but I have a feeling that he's been reaping the consequences lately. He seems aimless and hurt."

"Hurt? By whom?"

"You." She shrugged. "Me. The world. I'm getting the feeling that he's afraid of something, too. You should try to help him."

Lora's words made much sense. They brought back feelings of guilt and loss. How many times in his life had he dropped everything to try to save him? He'd run to his defense in the classroom and on the playground. After church and at home. But all he'd gotten for it was pain and abuse.

Wasn't it right that he was putting himself first now? "I don't know how I can help him anymore. We're too different."

"You may be Amish and he's English, but that doesn't mean you can't love him still. You're brothers."

"I don't care that he's English. I don't even care that he didn't try to stay in touch after he left. But I can't be all right with the choices he's made."

Her open expression shuttered. "Well, now I understand."

"Do you?" he scoffed. "I kind of doubt it."

"You don't know what it was like, leaving the Amish like we did. Trying to make our way in the world when we had no idea what to do," Lora retorted. "It was hard, Mark."

"Life is hard. It don't matter what choices a person makes, if you make the choice to live, chances are better than good that each day ain't going to be easy."

Lora shook her head in obvious distaste. "No wonder Calvin never wanted to come back here. You are so sanctimonious."

"At least I'm not a drug addict."

"Oh, good point. Thank goodness you never did drugs. All you've done is beat women."

Mark felt his face and neck flush. He fought to show reaction, though he feared he was failing miserably. She'd struck a nerve, and they both knew it.

Before their conversation descended into an even lower level, he said, "I think it's time you left. Calvin ain't here and we have nothing to say to each other."

"*Jah*, I'll leave. But if I were you, I'd take care throwing all those stones of yours. One day someone is going to throw one back at ya. And it's going to hurt something awful."

Looking at her retreating form, Mark was fairly sure that he'd already had plenty of stones thrown his way. He knew because they truly had hurt. He had the scars to prove it.

As he went back inside, he pulled out his pocket watch and cursed under his breath. He now had less than fifteen minutes to shower and get to Waneta's house.

Food and prayer were going to have to come later.

Sometime much later.

Chapter 19

Wednesday night, August 10

Waneta, I swept the porch and wiped down the railing out there, too," her mother said. "At least Mark will think we keep a clean house."

With exaggerated patience, Waneta said, "Mark has already been outside on the porch. He's not going to care how clean everything is."

Pressing her hands on her waist, her mother looked at her with a knowing expression. "He might, daughter. Men like clean houses, you know."

As if women did not.

It was all so silly. Honestly, her mother was acting as if she'd never had a man come courting before. She had. Several men from their community had sat on her front porch swing over the last few years. She'd never been as anxious about their visits as she was about Mark's, though.

Hmm. Maybe her mother wasn't acting all that out of sorts, after all.

Then, as she scanned the dining room table and saw two platters filled with snacks and cookies, a pitcher of freshly squeezed lemonade, and a carafe of freshly brewed coffee, Neeta knew she hadn't been wrong. This was too much. Mark was going to be overwhelmed and she was going to be embarrassed.

"Mamm, he's coming over to sit on the porch swing. Not eat supper," she chided.

"He's a young man living by himself. Of course he's going to want some food."

"She ain't wrong!" Daed called out.

When her mother smiled at her, obviously pleased to have her opinion reinforced, Waneta gave in. There was nothing she could do about the refreshments now anyway.

"It does look real nice, Mamm. Thank you for going to so much trouble. I'm worried that you overdid it, though. You know how you get tired when you overexert yourself."

"Bustling around the *haus* from time to time is good for me." Clasping her hands together, she said, "Now, what are you going to talk about with Mark?"

Oh, but her mother was chewing on her last nerve. "I don't know. Whatever comes to mind, I expect."

"I think you should have something better in mind. Don't you?" She nodded encouragingly.

That was her mother's favorite habit. She asked questions in conjunction with either a nod or a shake of the head. When she was younger, Neeta had appreciated the signals; it gave her a very good idea about what response would make her mother happiest.

But now she only felt the not-so-subtle movements were rather amusing. "Mamm, I'm not going to have conversation starters prepared in my head for Mark. We work all day together and get along just fine." Okay, that was probably a bit of an exaggeration, but it was still true.

"Well, whatever you do, don't talk about work," she warned.

"Why not?"

"Because work isn't romantic."

That was true. Work definitely was not romantic. But she wasn't about to guide the conversation toward romance! "Daed, help me out here," she called.

"Sorry, Waneta, but I'm helpless when it comes to the ways of courting."

"Not really. You courted Mamm."

"*Nee*, it was more like I was wandering around town when your mother snagged me. I didn't stand a chance."

Snagged? Her seventy-two-year-old father just admitted that her mother snagged him?

"Oh! He's here!" Mamm said, smiling from her spot next to the front windows.

Sure enough, two raps accompanied her mother's announcement. Mark had arrived. And not a moment too soon.

"I'll get the door, Mamm," she said as she turned the knob. Hopefully, her mother would take the hint and leave before she said anything to embarrass Waneta.

"Hey, Waneta," Mark said. "I'm sorry I'm late."

"Nothing to apologize for. I didn't even notice the time."

"She means that in the best way possible, Mark," Mamm said over her shoulder.

"Mother—"

But instead of looking as uncomfortable as Waneta felt, Mark just grinned. "That's *gut* to know, Mrs. Cain. Otherwise, a man might be feeling a bit forgettable."

"Want some food?" Daed called from his easy chair. "Gettie's been cooking all afternoon for ya."

His expression went blank. "You have?"

It was too much. They were being so heavy-handed, he'd probably never come back. "You don't have to eat anything, Mark," she said quickly. "My mother just sometimes overdoes things."

"Actually, if you don't mind, I'd love something to eat. I'm starving. I didn't have time for dinner."

Giving Waneta a knowing look, her mother stepped closer. "Let me take you to the dining room and get you a plate."

"*Danke.*" After sending an apologetic look

Waneta's way, Mark walked to her mother's side.

When she was alone in the entryway, Waneta wondered what had come over her mother. Just a week or so ago she was gossiping about Mark and wanting Waneta to quit her job. Now she was practically planning their wedding. Had he really made such an impression on her when he visited?

Or, had Mamm truly taken Preacher Eli's words to heart and was practicing what he preached?

She was still dwelling on the changes when Mark came back out with a glass of lemonade in one hand and an overflowing plate in the other.

"Sorry about that," he said. "I really was hungry, though."

Now she was the one who was feeling like she needed to offer up an apology. "Nothing to apologize for," she said. "You just made my mother happy. And I wouldn't have wanted you to sit on the porch with me swinging while your stomach was growling."

"This is going to be the best meal I've had since, well, the last time I was here."

She laughed. "My mother is a fine cook. I'll pass on your appreciation."

Mark sat down with his plate of fried chicken, sauerkraut balls, pickles, and cheese and crackers. After chomping down on one of the pickles, he said, "I don't know what happened. The time got away from me."

"What were you doing?"

"I've been pulling up old linoleum. Then I had an unexpected guest."

"Was it your brother again?"

"*Nee.* Lora Weaver."

"Lora? What did she want?"

"To talk about my brother." Looking down at his plate, he ate another couple of pieces of chicken, then said, "Do you mind if we don't talk about either of them right now? I need a break."

Though she nodded, Waneta couldn't deny that she was feeling awkward all over again. It looked like he still didn't trust her. Why had he even wanted to come over if he didn't feel comfortable answering even the easiest question?

Minutes later, his plate was cleared. He stood up and rested it on the small table on the corner of the porch. After sipping his lemonade, he eyed her warily.

"Did I just make a mess of things?"

"By eating? Of course not."

"By everything. Inhaling my food. Showing up late. By doing what I just did."

"You've lost me, Mark. I don't know what you are referring to."

"Because I didn't explain myself. You look hurt."

"That's not how I'm feeling. I'm . . . well, I'm wondering what we should talk about."

"Anything you want to talk about is fine."

"Except your brother. Or Lora's visit. Or why the sheriff wanted to talk to you. Or Amy Miller's attack."

"You're right. I have a lot to learn about conversation. I promise I'm trying, though."

Remembering Amy's parting words about acting holier than thou, Waneta said, "I have things I'm working on, too, Mark."

His gaze warmed. It was obvious that he was grateful that she had let him off so easy. Kicking one of his legs out, he said, "So, did you end up going over to see Amy?"

"I did."

"I'm sure you brought her a lot of comfort."

"Not so much. We ended up arguing."

"What about?"

"About her. Me. And some things that don't matter."

"I guess you are getting as good as I am about keeping things hidden."

"Not really," said Waneta. "Though, I am finding it hard to be open and honest with someone who doesn't want to act the same way. I wouldn't say you've been difficult. But you do have me confused."

"I'm not surprised. I have been prickly about a lot of things, haven't I?"

"Yes. But that's your business, Mark. Not mine."

"No. I said I really like you, but now I'm not hardly giving you anything back. Ask me anything and I'll try to answer as best I can."

She was disappointed. She felt like he was making her do the choosing about delving into his personal life. It hardly seemed fair.

Instead, she kicked her legs out and said, "I remember when I was twelve and you were sixteen."

"Let's see. That means I was out of school and working for Henry."

"*Jah*. You were." She smiled softly. "I was walking home and was having quite a time carrying all of my things. I got to take Miss Edith's rat home for the weekend."

He chuckled. "I'd forgotten all about that rat. Everyone sure loved it."

"*Jah*. they did. I couldn't wait to be chosen to be the lucky girl who got to take the rat home. Anyway, when my weekend came, I had my hands full on the way home. I had a time juggling it all and kept stopping to catch my breath and rearrange my books, that cage, and my lunch pail. Then, just when you walked by, everything but the rat tumbled to the ground."

Remembering the moment as if it was yesterday, she looked at him. "I was so frustrated with myself and embarrassed, I almost started crying. But all you did was kneel down, pick up all my books, and offer to see me home."

"I wish I could tell you that I remember that afternoon, but I don't." Looking off into the distance, he said, "I'm even trying to remember why I would have been walking along that road at that time, when I was sixteen."

"It was because of Calvin. You used to walk Calvin home, which he constantly complained about."

"Oh, yeah." Looking reflective, he said, "I remember that day now. Calvin had just run off a couple of days before. I had forgotten until I watched everyone walk out the schoolhouse door and he didn't appear." Smiling at her, he said, "I didn't think you were ever going to let me hold that cage, Waneta."

"I didn't want you to. I thought you would take it from me."

"You thought I'd steal it?"

Oh, but he sounded indignant! "Maybe," she teased. "All I could think about was how much everyone else had wanted to take the creature home. But I was the one Miss Edith had picked."

He laughed. "Miss Edith would have never let Calvin or me take it home. She didn't trust us."

"With good reason. You took pencils."

He shrugged. "We needed pencils. It weren't like our father was going to spend his money on school supplies. Miss Edith knew that, too, but she never seemed to care."

Waneta gulped. This conversation strand wasn't going well, either. It was time to get to the point. "The reason I brought it up was because you said something to me when we were walking side by side."

"What did I say that was worth remembering?"

"You said that you'd never met another girl who tried so hard to be good." She was somewhat pleased that her voice didn't tremble when she said that.

But instead of looking touched by the memory, he pressed a palm to his face. Like he was embarrassed. "I was a jerk."

"You were a jerk a lot of the time, Mark," she agreed. "But not then. That day? You were kind. You also told me that the rat was probably going to have the best weekend of its life with me."

The corners of his mouth lifted. "I bet I wasn't wrong."

"I don't know if you were right or wrong. What's important is that I didn't understand what you meant back then. I do now. It was a lovely compliment."

"You are a nice person, Waneta. You've always been that way. You've got a good heart."

"You do, too."

"Not really."

"Why did you come back, Mark? Was it really because of the house?"

"Partly. But also because of Henry. He got a talking-to from his physician. The man said

Henry ain't resting enough and needed to stop trying to do too much."

"So you came to help."

"I did. I know he appreciates you, Waneta, but he needs someone to take care of the hard labor and the heavy lifting. I aim to get him to let me do more and more as the weeks go by. I'm hoping that soon he'll only work a couple of days a week."

"He must be so glad you came back to help him."

"So far, I don't think so. Since I've come back, I've gotten the impression that everything around Horse Cave has started to fall apart."

"Hardly."

"Amy Miller was just attacked." He raised his eyebrows. "That wasn't good."

"I agree. But just because something awful happened since you returned doesn't mean we haven't had our share of drama around here from time to time. Believe me, bad things have happened in the county even when you were gone. Why, a girl was kidnapped and tied up in a basement over in Munfordville a couple of months ago!"

He sighed. "I hear you. But I still feel like I've given Henry a new set of problems."

"Even if you have, I hope you won't add them to your burdens. I think Henry can handle most anything."

"I think he can, too. But that doesn't mean he should have to." Mark took a deep breath. "Waneta, when Calvin showed up at Blooms and Berries, I was very upset."

She could tell that he was really struggling to hold on to his composure. And that he was trying his best to reveal his feelings in an honest and forthright way. It made her want to try to help him as much as she could, even though she feared she was hopelessly incapable of really helping a man who'd already suffered through so many personal tragedies.

"That was understandable," she said slowly. "You didn't want to see him."

"You're right. I didn't. And though that is something I haven't quite come to terms with, it wasn't the only reason I was angry with him." After taking a deep breath, he said, "It was because he was playing with me. Playing with all of us. I hate that he is involving you in his games."

"How so?"

"He could have come to the house at any time. But he was picking to come to the nursery because he wanted you and Henry to see him. He wanted other customers to see me talking to him."

"Why would he care about that?"

"He doesn't want to see me. He only wants me to sell the house and give him half the money."

"Would you do that?"

"On my good days, I think of course not. I don't want to leave. On my not so good days, I think that selling the house wouldn't solve either of our problems."

"And on others?"

"On other days? I want to pack up my duffel and take off. Get as far away from here as I possibly can."

"I hope you don't do that."

Some of the chill faded from his eyes. "You really mean that, don't you?"

"I do." After weighing what she was about to say for a moment, she decided to simply speak her mind. "Forgive me, but I think there's another reason you came back here, Mark. I think the Lord needed you to come back and deal with all the hurts and problems that have been plaguing you for so long. I think He knows you won't really be happy until you are able to look your brother, your house, and everyone who was so quick to judge you in the eye."

"That's easy to suggest but a lot harder to do."

She was just relieved he hadn't thrown her suggestion back in her face. "I bet it is," she agreed easily.

"And what do you think I should say to everyone? What do you think I should say to Calvin when I talk to him again?"

"I canna answer that." Even she knew one

couldn't tell someone else that they needed to accept their apology or grant forgiveness. That had to be something that was decided on all by oneself.

"Waneta. You canna just offer me some advice? Tell me what you really think I should do."

"I don't know what words you need to say. But more importantly, I don't think I'm supposed to know them. Only you and God know." She squirmed under his gaze. "I know I'm probably not helping, but I wanted to tell you what I thought. I really do think God has brought you back here to heal."

His gaze sharpened. "What about you?"

"Me?"

"*Jah*. If the Lord wants me to see all the people I hoped I never saw again, and to make peace with them, too . . . what do you think He wants me to do with people like you?"

"Like me?" She could practically feel her skin turning a deep shade of pink.

"*Jah*," he murmured, still staring at her intently. "Waneta, do you think I should follow my instinct and see where our relationship leads? Or—" He stopped abruptly.

But she needed to hear his thoughts. "Or?"

"Or wait until everything in my life is peaceful again?"

She felt deflated and more than a little let down. "Mark, when you say things like that,

I always find it confusing. I never know if you are teasing or being completely serious."

"I'm serious. I wouldn't joke about you and me."

"You sound mighty sure about that."

"I am. I waited too long to have a moment like this. There's no way I'm going to give it up without a fight."

She wasn't sure if he thought *she* would be fighting him or if everyone around them would.

But maybe it didn't matter. All that did matter was that they were now trusting each other enough to build the beginnings of a relationship.

That in itself was something for which to be grateful.

Chapter 20

Thursday, August 11

He was in her station. Standing over by one of the back counters.

Lora studied Deputy Beck. He was dressed in a pair of faded jeans that were frayed at the edges, flip-flops, and a snug-fitting weathered gray T-shirt. He looked far different than he did in his usual khaki-colored uniform. Younger. Maybe even more approachable.

Bill's wife, Mia, had just seated him in one of the booths by the west wall. He was halfheartedly looking at the menu. And far more intently looking around the diner.

Instinctively, Lora knew he was looking for her.

The question, of course, was why. Had he felt the same little zing of awareness that she'd felt every time they'd talked as well? Or had something else happened and he needed to ask her about it?

"Are you going to go wait on our customer, Lora, or expect him to serve himself?" Bill said from the other side of the kitchen window.

"I'm going. Sorry, Bill."

"No apology needed. That just ain't like you, watching and waiting. You are usually far more eager."

She couldn't deny that. While most of the other girls who worked there were always dreaming about the day they worked somewhere else, Lora actually liked her job.

Here, at Bill's Diner, she'd found a home of sorts. Bill and Mia were good to her, making her feel like she mattered to them. She also felt a lot of pride in her work. At Bill's she felt in control. She knew how to manage her time and how to manage her customers. She was good at waitressing, too. She always got the most tips and the most requests from regulars for her section.

The other girls said it was because of her usual attire of snug tank tops and the way her dark-blond hair hung in waves down her back.

Lora knew her popularity was because she took care of her customers. Young or old, Amish or English, local or tourist, she made it her mission to make sure they were glad they'd come to Bill's.

Which was why it really wasn't like her to keep Deputy Beck waiting.

Grabbing a pitcher of water, she hurried over to him. "Hey, Deputy Beck. I'm sorry I kept you waiting. I guess I was asleep on my feet. Water?"

"Sure." He smiled up at her as she poured. "How are you today?"

"Just fine. You?"

"Not exactly terrific, but I'm all right, too."

His honesty made some of her professional armor falter. "I hope everything is okay."

"It will be." He smiled again. This time the corners of his eyes crinkled a bit.

She tried not to be affected. "Do you know what you want to order?"

"I can't decide." Studying the menu, he said, "What is your favorite? The tuna melt or the cheeseburger?"

"Both are good."

"Which one do you eat more often?"

"Neither of them. I usually get a salad or something."

"Ah. You're a healthy eater."

When did his order become centered around her? "I'm a girl who likes fitting into her jeans."

Lowering his menu, he slowly eyed her from head to toe. "I guess a server here does have to practice some serious willpower."

"If I didn't, I'd gain ten pounds every month."

"Nah, you'd just have to go running with me every morning."

It sounded like he was turning their acquaintance into a relationship. And the way he was smiling at her! It was so direct. Just like she meant something to him.

Nervously, she glanced behind her, hoping none of the other girls heard him talk to her like that.

She wouldn't live it down for weeks. "Deputy, most people really like Bill's cheeseburgers. I don't think you could go wrong there."

"I'll have one of those, then. And a strawberry shake." He winked. "I'm living on the edge today."

In spite of how agitated she felt around him, she laughed. "I'll get that order in and bring you your shake in a jiffy."

"Thanks." He smiled, then started fussing with his cell phone.

When she turned, Lora realized her fears had come true. She'd been watched. The other servers, Mia, and Bill had watched the interplay between her and the deputy. All four of them were grinning like Christmas had come early.

Ignoring their speculative glances, Lora rushed back and turned in the order, then started scooping ice cream for the shake.

But just as she had known it would happen, Meredith joined her at the counter. "Boy, he never talks to me like that when I take his order."

"Maybe he's in a chatty mood today," Lora replied, hoping she sounded far calmer than she felt.

Then Christine came over, too, turned, and stared at him boldly. "Do you know him?"

No way was she going to share that he'd questioned her. "Kind of." As she added strawberry powder and a cup of milk to the blender, she lowered her voice. "Turn around, would you?"

Christine did as Lora asked. "What does 'kind of' mean? Have y'all gone out? Are you dating?"

If Lora had been sipping water, she would have choked on it. "No."

"Do you want to? Because it sure looks like he does."

Feeling even more flustered, Lora jabbed at one of the buttons on the blender. "I need to get this out to him and check on my other customers."

Meredith chuckled. "Okay. I get the hint. I was just going to tell you that I hoped you were. You'd make a cute couple."

If she only knew! Quickly, she poured the mixture into a tall glass and brought it to the deputy. "Enjoy the shake. Your burger should be up soon."

"No hurry. I'm fine just sitting here."

Lora smiled weakly as she checked on her three other customers, collected a tip from a fourth, and helped get the door for a mom holding a cranky toddler.

"Order up," Bill called out.

Getting the deputy's plate, she brought it to him. "Here you go, Deputy Beck. Enjoy."

"Any chance you can sit with me for a sec?"

"I'm working."

"I know. But if you get a break or something?"

Dread settled in. "Did anything else happen?"

"Beyond Amy Miller getting attacked? No."
Looking at her intently, he said, "See if you can take a break, though, would you?"

In spite of herself, she nodded. Unsure of what to do, she checked on her only other customer, an older man who was one of her regulars. As usual, he was eating a dish of chicken fried steak while reading his book. Other than making sure his glass of iced tea was filled, he wasn't going to need anything for at least another fifteen minutes.

"Go sit down," Mia said.

Looking at her boss's wife, she sighed. "You heard?"

"Christine did, who informed me," she whispered. "Now, go sit down and take a break for fifteen. I'll keep an eye on Mr. Granger."

Out of excuses, Lora walked back to Deputy Beck's booth and sat down. He was about halfway through his cheeseburger. When he looked up at her, she smiled awkwardly. "I decided to take that break now. I have fifteen minutes."

"Good." After sipping some water, he leaned back against the red vinyl seat. "I wanted to see how you've been doing since we talked."

She shrugged. "I've been all right."

"Honestly?"

"Deputy Beck, I'm not sure how to answer you. Are you here on business? Am I in trouble?"

"I'm here because I care how you're doing."

But why? "Well, in that case, I guess you could say I'm doing about as well as can be expected after embarrassing myself with Calvin Fisher."

"That's kind of a strange way of putting it."

"I hate that I let a couple of brothers make me feel so bad about myself that I relapsed. I'm stronger than that."

"*Both* Calvin and Mark?" Looking concerned, he said, "Was Mark at your house, too?"

"Oh, no," she said in a rush, wishing that she'd taken the time to think how her words were going to sound. "Mark didn't do anything. He just . . . Well, he reminded me that I was a lot different than him." And the perpetually perfect Waneta Cain. Practically squirming in her seat, she said, "As for Calvin? He was being like he always was—trouble. I simply allowed myself not to care for a couple of hours one evening." Pressing a hand to her cheek, she said, "I learned my lesson, though. And, before you ask, no, I haven't seen him since."

He studied her as he took another bite, chewed thoughtfully, then sipped the last of his shake. "You know, I actually didn't intend to talk about all that."

"What did you intend to discuss?"

"I don't know." He smiled suddenly. "Me? You? I was hoping I could find a way to get you to relax a little bit more around me. Then I could ask you out."

"Like on a date?" Oh, no. Had she just said that?

Grinning now, he nodded. "Guess I'm pretty bad at this, huh?"

"If you're bad at it, I'm worse. I don't have a lot of experience dating." She didn't have any experience with men doing the stuff they did in movies and books, where they picked her up at her front door and treated her like she was worth their time and money.

"Will you think about it?"

"Yes."

Looking pleased, he said, "In the meantime, I'm going to plan to have a bunch of meals here. Maybe I'll even try that tuna melt next time I come in. And a chocolate shake, too."

"If you keep eating like that, you're going to have to run morning and night."

"That's okay. I still haven't given up hope that I'll have company. Now, here's a question for you. How many times have you actually been inside Horse Cave?"

The sudden switch of topics made her laugh. As they chatted, his questions about the cave and the surrounding areas encouraged her to think about a lot of things she usually took for granted. Newcomers to the area were often surprised to learn that their town was actually built on top of an actual cavern.

"I've only been inside twice."

"That's it?"

"It was enough. It's not like Mammoth Cave; it's a dark and wet place."

Eddie frowned. "How come?"

She laughed again as she told him what she knew about the cave's history . . . even the rumors about how it got its name from outlaws who hid their horses deep inside. Eddie listened with interest, asking her all kinds of questions. Making her feel like she was interesting.

Later, when he left, she realized she'd never take conversations like that for granted again. They were too sweet. Too special.

Chapter 21

Thursday, August 11

Mark had now called on Waneta Cain two times in two days. This visit had been just as successful as the first.

Almost becoming a habit.

"Come back soon, Mark," Gettie called out from her front door, waving like she was saying good-bye to a long-lost relative. "Don't be a stranger."

Feeling a bit like he'd stepped into another man's life, Mark returned her wave, smiled at Waneta, then started home. In his arms were two bags of food. One was filled with leftovers from today's visit; in the other, a block of white cheddar cheese and a loaf of freshly baked bread.

"Everyone can do with fresh baked bread and some cheese from S&L Salvage, don'tcha think?" Gettie had said when she'd placed the bounty of food in his arms.

Overwhelmed by such kindness, he'd mumbled a barely coherent response. "*Danke.* I will enjoy everything."

"I know you will. You need to eat more, Mark."

Biting his lip, he turned to meet Waneta's eyes. They were bright with amusement. She shrugged and smiled.

After thanking Mrs. Cain again, he collected the items with pleasure. He was going to have fresh bread later that night, and a couple more cookies, too. Such food could never be taken for granted.

Now, as he walked along the street, he allowed himself to remember another time when he'd gotten such a gift. It had been when he was still a child, probably no more than eight or nine. It was the last day of school before Christmas break and everyone in the classroom had been so excited about the upcoming days off.

Everyone but him, he'd thought. Calvin had still been young enough to be hopeful about Christmas. He still believed that their parents were going to up and change and suddenly act like the other children's parents. Though Mark knew that wasn't going to be the case, he hadn't had the heart to burst Calvin's bubble. All it would do was make him sad and whiney, and Mark had enough to do without dealing with that, too.

Because of all that, at the end of the day he was the last child to leave the classroom. Just as he was putting on his coat, Waneta's mother walked inside.

"Mark," she'd said. "I'm so glad you are still here."

"How come?" he'd asked.

Her smile widened. "Because I have something for you." She held out a canvas bag with a little Velcro flap on it.

He'd taken it suspiciously. "What is it?"

"I made you some cookies and granola bars."

Opening up the flap, he saw at least two dozen individually wrapped snacks. The scent of chocolate, brown sugar, and molasses made his stomach growl. He knew that if he only ate one or two a day, he could make them last for the whole break. He could hide the bag in his backpack. No one would look in there and they'd be his secret.

But something felt strange about accepting it. "Did you bring everyone a bag?"

"*Nee*, Mark. Only you and Calvin."

"Did you already give Calvin his bag?"

"*Nee*." Looking at him directly in the eye, she said, "I thought you might want to give it to him later. Maybe on your way home."

Mark knew if Calvin got a tote filled with snacks, the first thing he'd do would be to tell their parents. Their *mamm* would probably just look at it in confusion.

But their father would be angry. He'd use it as a reason to get mad at the both of them. Would likely say that they'd been bellyaching about their home to the teacher or to the other kids.

Then they'd no doubt get punished.

He knew what he had to do. "I don't want them," he said, before walking out the school-house door.

He could feel Mrs. Cain's disappointed look resting on his back, but he didn't pause to say anything. It was better if she thought he was mean and rude. That was better instead of poor and hungry.

"You ready, Calvin?" he'd asked, his voice sounding gruff, even to his own ears.

"*Jah.*" With a smile, Calvin trotted to his side. "Guess what? Some of the kids said when they get home, they're gonna have hot chocolate and popcorn, on account of it being the last day of school before Christmas."

"Good for them."

Calvin scampered a bit to keep up with Mark's stride. "Do you think Mamm will have that waiting for us?"

"*Nee.*"

His brother's eager smile faltered. "You sure? Maybe—"

"That ain't how things are at our *haus*. You know that, Calvin. Don't pretend otherwise."

When Calvin's steps slowed, Mark breathed a sigh of relief. It was better this way. Better for Calvin to stop hoping for things that were never going to happen.

Mark shook off the memory, hating how it made him feel. If he could go back in time, he would have taken the cookies, of course. At the very least they could have eaten a bunch of them on the way home.

All refusing had done was make him sadder and angrier at the world. It hadn't changed one thing about his life.

When Mark walked in his front door, he half expected someone else to be waiting for him. That seemed to be the case these days. People were popping up out of his past without notice. Causing him to react without thought.

However, the house was quiet. It was also dark, thanks to the fading sunlight outside. After lighting a kerosene lantern, he set the tote bags on one of the kitchen countertops and opened one of the windows that had a screen, just to encourage some fresh air.

Then he walked through each room in the house to make sure there were no signs of visitors while he'd been gone.

But like the kitchen, everything seemed peaceful and didn't look disturbed. He sat down on his bed and removed his heavy boots and socks. Then wiggled his toes, glad to feel the cool, smooth wood underfoot.

Feeling relaxed, he walked back into the living room and sat down in the lone chair there.

The chair was new. He'd probably paid too much for it. He should have either kept the furniture that his father had left behind, or bought something at a thrift store. But he hadn't been able to.

Actually, keeping the furniture that had been left behind hadn't even been a possibility. It reminded him too much of long evenings spent watching his father either drink or smoke himself into a stupor. Or of him standing in front of the chair while his father sat and yelled, blaming him for Calvin's leaving and his *mamm's* taking off.

No, he told himself sternly. One trip down memory lane was more than enough for one afternoon. He needed to concentrate on something else. Anything else.

But when he heard the footsteps at the front door, he stood up with a sense of relief.

It seemed he wouldn't be alone with his memories for the time being after all.

Opening the door, he braced himself for whoever was there.

But when he saw Preacher Eli, he couldn't have been more surprised. Instead of greeting him right away, he stood and gaped at him in confusion.

Preacher Eli was only three or four years older than himself. He'd grown up in Charm, Ohio, and had moved to Hart County when he was twenty-one or twenty-two. His and his wife's families had helped them buy some rich farm-land, the price of property being much less in central Kentucky than in northern Ohio. Since then, Eli had been a farmer and a popular member of the community.

Mark heard he'd become a preacher only the year before. It seemed that the Lord had been very wise when He'd guided Eli to be called. Eli was a gifted preacher and a kind man.

But Mark had never heard of him doing evening house calls.

"Is everything all right?" Mark said at last.

"Of course. I just decided to pay you a visit. I'm glad I caught you at home. I wasn't sure if you were inside. It looked mighty quiet."

"I just got home, as a matter of fact. Would you like to come in?"

"I would."

Little by little, good manners returned. He waved a hand inside. "Do you want coffee or a glass of water?"

"Water sounds good. *Danke*."

When Mark turned to go to the kitchen, the preacher followed. Whistling softly, he said, "My, look at the floors. They are going to be very fine."

"I hope so. They're gonna take a lot of work, but they'll be worth it," he said as he got them both glasses of water.

"Are you planning to work on them this week? If so, I could come by with two or three men from my cousin's shop and help you prep them."

"Thank you. I would appreciate that," he murmured. It felt a bit strange to accept such help so quickly, but he couldn't think of refusing. Not when there was so much to do. "I had forgotten that some of your family owns a woodworking shop."

"One by one, we're all moving out here. We like Kentucky. I like to do carpentry from time to time as well. It makes for a nice change in routine from my usual preaching and farming."

Mark had always thought it would be mighty hard to be a preacher. Names were drawn by lots, and the job was assigned for the rest of a man's life. "The Lord has blessed you, for sure."

"He's blessed us all." Preacher Eli took a chair and stretched his legs out. "I came over to see how you were doing. Are you having a difficult time being back here?"

Well, that was surely blunt. But what could he say? "*Jah.*"

Preacher Eli's eyebrows raised before he broke into a broad grin. "I'm glad you don't mind speaking the truth."

"You might not say that in a few minutes. I'm afraid it's been quite a trying day. I think I don't have any more space in my head to phrase things gently."

"It's my lucky day, then. 'Cause I surely didn't come over here for you to keep your answers from me."

"What questions do you have?" asked Mark.

"I'd like to know how I can help make your return easier."

"I'm not sure how you can do that. Not with Amy hurt and her boyfriend telling anyone who will listen that I attacked her."

Preacher Eli looked down at his folded hands. "Abraham is a hothead, to be sure," he said after taking a fortifying breath. "He's a bit confused these days, too."

"He ain't confused about his feelings for me. Everyone is talking about how Abraham thinks I attacked her."

"He's worried about his girl. When he settles down, his harsh words will, too." Before Mark could argue that point, Eli said, "Now, what about everything else? Are you liking your job?"

"*Jah.* I like it fine. Henry Lehmann is a good man."

"He's in poor health, though," said the preacher. "He tries to cover up his pain, but I fear it is getting worse."

Mark nodded. "I'm worried about that, too. I'm glad I'm there to help him."

"And to be with Waneta Cain, too, *jah*?"

Eli was a wily man, to be sure. Just as Mark had relaxed, he'd circled back to the one person who had him completely in knots. He would have appreciated being able to have this time to think about his feelings for her and keep them to himself.

But maybe that was the problem with his life at the moment? He was so conditioned to getting hurt, he kept everything to himself. That didn't solve all his problems, though. It made him seem unreachable to everyone that he thought he was trying to befriend.

He needed to let down his guard and share his worries and weaknesses. Only then would other people begin to trust him.

However, it wasn't easy. "I don't know what to say about Waneta," he said at last. It wasn't a great start, but at least he was trying.

Instead of letting Mark lead the conversation, Eli simply laughed. "There's nothing to say about Waneta, Mark. She is a lovely and faithful woman. That is enough to know about anyone. Ain't so?"

Not necessarily. "She is also too trusting."

"Of whom? You?"

That was exactly what he feared. "Maybe."

Eli reached out and squeezed his shoulder. "Mark, I am going to offer some advice. I'd like you to listen, but you don't have to accept it. Okay?"

He nodded.

Looking pleased, Eli leaned back in his chair. "Here's the thing. You can't walk backwards all your life. You also canna get very far if you are constantly looking over your shoulder and wondering if anyone is following you."

"I know no one is following me." That was part of his problem.

But instead of smiling, Eli's light-brown eyes narrowed. "You could not control what your parents did. You could not control how your father treated you. Or your brother."

That went against everything he'd been fighting. "But—"

"*Nee*. No buts. You need to come to terms with this, Mark, or it's going to eat you up inside. The fact of the matter is that you also could not help Calvin."

"You weren't around then. You don't know. He was only fourteen when he took off."

"I realize I came after he left, but I remember the pain in your eyes—even all these years later. I have talked and prayed with the other preachers in the area about you and your family, too."

While Mark attempted to process that, Eli continued. "You were only sixteen, Mark," he said, each word emphasized. "You were only sixteen. You were not a man. You were not in control. Stop carrying that guilt."

Stop carrying that guilt. Four words. Forcibly said. He swallowed hard. "Is that what you think I've been doing?"

"*Nee*. That's what I *know* you've been doing. You've been secretly apologizing for all kinds of things that weren't your fault and you had no control over." He stood up then.

Eli's relatively small stature—he was only five foot seven compared to Mark's six foot two frame—seemed to grow in size as he looked down at Mark. "You did not hurt Bethany Williams. You did not attack her. You did not attempt to rape her."

"I know that. I've been telling everyone that, too. But—"

"But you have acted like a man who was ashamed."

"I was ashamed of who I was," he said with some surprise.

"You are a survivor. You don't give up. You have a good heart. You are a good person. You are someone worth knowing."

"Thank you."

"*Nee*. Don't thank me for seeing the real you," Eli said with obvious impatience. "Go out in the world and let everyone else see the real you, too."

"Including Waneta . . ." *There.*

He finally got it.

But Preacher Eli shook his head. "*Nee*. Not including Waneta. She already sees the real you. That's why she trusts you and wants to be with you. I mean everyone else."

Everyone else. The entire population of Horse Cave. Everyone in Hart County. Even, it seemed, Calvin.

Feeling vulnerable, Mark said, "My brother came back. He wants me to sell the house and give him some money."

"Do you want to do that?"

"*Nee*. I want to continue fixing it up. Make it livable. It will be a nice place to live in eventually."

"I agree. It's big enough for a family, too."

"But Calvin might have a point. The house is half his, after all."

"Why is it half his? Because he was born?"

"Well, yes." Mark thought that was pretty obvious. "I mean, that's what is fair."

"But you've already learned that life isn't fair, right?"

"To be sure."

"Then why do you need to bend over backwards to help a man who doesn't have any interest in helping you even a little?"

Mark gaped. "That seems kind of harsh."

"I agree. It does. But that doesn't mean I'm wrong."

His bluntness hurt. But maybe Eli was correct. Everything that was right didn't always feel comforting. Standing up, Mark said, "Eli, this visit of yours sure packs a wallop. I feel a bit run over and damaged."

"I didn't mean to do that. But I did want to wake you up." Pointing to the window, he said, "There's a big world out there. It is filled with pain and hurt. To be sure. But it's also filled with opportunities and wonderful people. And love. If you dare to step out of your prison."

With those cryptic words still ringing in Mark's ears, Eli said, "Well now. I had better get on my way. I have one more visit to go before the sun disappears completely."

Walking him to the door, Mark said, "Hey, Eli?"

Eli paused. "*Jah*?"

"God knew what He was doing when He made you a preacher. You have a gift."

Eli smiled, his eyes lighting up, too. "*Danke*, Mark. Our Lord is good, to be sure. I am blessed that He has entrusted me with so much."

At the door then, Preacher Eli took his hat and left.

Leaving Mark feeling exhausted and energized, and with four words still ringing in his ears. *Stop carrying the guilt.*

He'd definitely needed to hear that, he realized as he went into the kitchen, unwrapped the block of cheese he'd brought home, and sliced a thick wedge. Then he sliced a piece of Gettie Cain's homemade bread. After making a small sandwich, he took a bite.

It tasted good. Tasted perfect.

And, perhaps, like he deserved it, too.

Chapter 22

Mark had asked to come in late, and Mr. Lehmann had already shared that he wouldn't be working until early afternoon. He had a couple of doctors' appointments over in Bowling Green.

Therefore, Waneta was working at the nursery by herself. It was an unusual occurrence. Usually, her boss asked one of the younger boys who worked on the weekends to join her, if for no other reason than to help customers with lifting bags of mulch and carrying plants and shrubs to their vehicles. But, today, he hadn't been able to find anyone to work. It seemed a lot of people were traveling this week.

Waneta didn't mind being at Blooms and Berries alone, however. Actually, she was kind of enjoying the novelty. Since she was so busy caring for her parents and the house in the evenings, it was a rare experience to have time for herself. This slow day at the nursery was a good opportunity to sort out some things in her head.

In between helping the few people who had

entered the store, Waneta had constructed mental lists of things to tackle and other things to leave to God.

The first item had been Amy Miller. Waneta had come to realize that she wasn't going to be able to change Amy's opinion about Mark anytime soon. Since she was not going to simply stay quiet while Amy bad-mouthed Mark, it was necessary to give Amy space to recover. It had been a hard decision. She liked Amy very much. But that didn't mean she had to listen to Amy's mean comments.

Was Amy the first of many people she was going to have to distance herself from if she continued to fight for Mark's character? She hoped not, but it might very well be the case.

When the door chimed, she lifted her head to smile at the newcomers, glad to take a break from her thoughts.

Just as quickly, she stifled a groan.

James and Katie Eicher had returned, and James looked just as irritated by life as he had the last time he was there.

Remembering Mr. Lehmann's words, about how it wasn't necessary to like every customer in order to serve them well, Waneta stepped forward to greet them.

"James. Katie. Good day," she said pleasantly.

Katie's eyes warmed. "*Gut* day to you, too, Waneta. Is it hot enough for you?"

Waneta lifted up her foot, showing off her yellow rubber flip-flops, which matched her pretty daffodil dress. "It's so hot I decided to give my feet a break today. It was too hot to even wear tennis shoes."

"I bet," Katie said with a small laugh. "I've considered wearing flip-flops a time or two myself."

"Except that it ain't seemly," James said.

"Of course, James," Katie murmured, all traces of laughter firmly tamped down.

Oh, that James was just so mean to his wife! With great effort, Waneta kept her voice friendly and even. "What can I help you two with?"

"You can find a man to assist me."

It was becoming harder and harder not to glare. "I'm sorry, there's only me right now."

James looked around the shop. "Where is Henry?"

"He's not in this morning." She didn't think it was everyone's business what Henry was doing. "Now, did you come in for anything special?"

"What about Mark Fisher? Is he here? Or, did Henry finally get rid of him?"

"Mark will be in later," she said with rapidly evaporating patience. "Now, I'll be happy to help you with whatever you are looking for . . ."

"He's still an employee? Even after what happened to Amy?"

Though she was tempted to jump to Mark's

236

defense, she kept her expression as neutral as possible. "Just let me know when you are ready for my assistance."

"I don't know what has gotten into everyone around here. First criminals are walking around unattended and now good Amish girls are running around, getting themselves into trouble."

That was the last straw. No longer caring if she was going to have to listen to one of Mr. Lehmann's lectures, Waneta pressed her hands to her hips. "Are you referring to Amy? I believe she was attacked near her house."

"If she was attacked there, it's only by chance. You know what she's become like. Wild."

"I saw her yesterday. She was hurt very bad. She most certainly didn't deserve what happened to her."

Katie rested her hand on James's bicep. "James, you know we didn't come in here to discuss Amy's accident."

Accident? Before she could stop herself, Waneta said, "I don't know if you could call her attack an accident. Some terrible man tried to rape her, you see."

James shook his arm free of his wife's clasp as he strode forward. "You don't know what you are talking about. I think you should stick to only discussing work."

That had been what she'd been trying to do! "I would rather you not speak to me that way."

"Good Amish girls are supposed to be biddable and demure. It's bad enough that you are working in a public place such as this. But now you are defending all sorts of people who shouldn't even be here."

"Are you saying that I'm not being a good person?"

He stepped forward, overwhelming her with his size. "I'm saying you should be watching yourself and being careful about who you speak to."

"Or what? What are you going to do?" Waneta asked, hardly aware that the door was opening.

"Or I'll make sure you will be disciplined."

Disciplined? She couldn't help it, she laughed. "James, what has gotten into you? Do you hear what you are—"

He grabbed her arm, yanked it hard. So hard, she knew her arm was going to be bruised and her shoulder was going to be sore. She cried out, "James!"

"Take your hand off of her," Mark called out as he rushed forward.

Instantly, James's hand lifted. He whirled around to face Mark. He stepped toward him, obviously looking anxious to fight.

But Mark ignored him. He walked right by James, moving with intent until he stopped directly in front of Waneta. "Are you all right?" he asked. "Has he hurt you?"

She realized then that she was trembling. "He didn't hurt me. But I'm glad you arrived. In the nick of time, too." She had the awful suspicion that James had been mere moments from doing something worse.

He rubbed her arm with his right hand. "I'm glad I got here when I did."

Just as she smiled at him, James's voice broke the moment.

"Look at you, Waneta. Standing there. Allowing him to touch you."

"You need to stop talking," Mark said. "Better yet, you need to leave. Immediately."

But James did not. "You've made your decision, haven't you, Waneta Cain?" he asked, his voice filled with sarcasm. "You've pushed aside what is right and proper. Instead, you've sided with the likes of him."

"James, I think it's time you left," a man who had entered the store called from the back of the room.

All of them turned.

Waneta breathed a sigh of relief. John Paul Schlabach and Matthew Yoder had just walked inside the shop and both of them were staring at James Eicher like he was the lowest sort of man.

"You watch it, John," James muttered.

John Paul strode forward, all two hundred and fifty pounds of him. "*No,* you watch it," he said. "You are causing a scene and frightening your *frau*. I don't know what is wrong with you, but I'm thinking you need to get your bearings. You're on the verge of losing control."

James froze as John walked to his side. "John Paul, you don't understand. Waneta here was acting uppity—"

"Now ain't the place," Matthew Yoder said as he moved to stand next to James on his other side. "Go on."

Without another word, Katie hurried toward the door. Her head was down and her shoulders slumped. She looked defeated.

Breathing like she'd just finished a marathon, Waneta watched Katie's departure. Part of her knew she should be feeling sorry for the woman, but she was too shaken by James's anger to feel much beyond relief. Her hands were shaking—her nerves were letting her know that the experience was taking its toll.

His hands in fists, James glared at all of them. "You are going to regret choosing a man like him over me." He turned to her again. "One day soon, when you are injured and hurt and lying on the ground forgotten, you will only have yourself to blame."

She was finding it difficult to breathe.

Moving closer to her side, Mark looked at him thoughtfully. "Are you threatening Waneta?"

"I don't need to threaten anyone," James countered, his expression triumphant. "I'm only predicting what will happen to any woman who trusts you. To any *person* who trusts you. You taint them. Hurt them. Always, sooner than later." With those parting words, he turned and walked out the door.

Waneta noticed that James's chin was up and his shoulders were pulled back. Just as if he'd made his point and he was proud about it.

The moment the door shut behind him, Waneta felt dizzy. "I need a minute," she mumbled as she hurried off to the storage room. She needed the dim, cool space in order to relax and regroup.

Once she was completely alone, she sank into one of the chairs. The tears that she had been holding at bay pricked her eyes as she wrapped her arms about herself. She had been really scared of one man in that room.

And it hadn't been Mark.

Chapter 23

Tuesday, August 16

As he sat in Lora Weaver's kitchen, with its pale turquoise walls, sparkling white counters, and worn-out table and chairs, Calvin Fisher was reflecting on things.

It was kind of a new thing but unavoidable.

Every time he had an extra minute or two, his mind would drift back to his most recent conversation with Mark. Over and over, he continually revisited the words they'd exchanged. It hadn't been pleasant.

Actually, it had been a painful undertaking. Few of the things that they'd discussed had made him feel good. Most of it had left him feeling empty and filled with pain.

From the time he left home at the age of fourteen, he'd taken care of himself. It hadn't been easy. He'd quickly learned that there were a whole lot of people in the world who enjoyed taking advantage of young Amish boys.

But he had prevailed. He'd worked odd jobs, learned how to manipulate people, learned to control situations in order to get what he needed.

He'd also gotten real good at imbibing a variety of substances so he wouldn't hurt too much. So he wouldn't feel too much. Numbness, whether it was derived from a six-pack of beer or a handful of pills, had its advantages.

Until he'd returned to Horse Cave, he hadn't thought much about the type of man he'd become or the significance of his actions. All he'd cared about was that he was surviving while so many others were not. But now, after talking to Mark and hearing his goals for the future, after witnessing the way he was slowly earning respect in a place where no one had ever respected their family, Calvin was beginning to wonder if he'd gotten it all wrong.

Maybe he should have cared more about consequences.

Maybe he should have tried harder to stay sober and forced himself to confront all of the demons in his past. If he had, he could be more like his brother right now.

Was it too late? He didn't know. He wondered if even God knew.

"Calvin!" Lora said around a yelp as she walked into her kitchen. "Oh my word. You scared me, sitting in here in the dark."

"Sorry. I didn't think you'd mind. I had nowhere else to go."

"Actually, I do mind. I don't want you coming inside without me being here. It ain't right."

She was wearing a simple sundress today. It was some kind of complicated floral pattern, all done in faded shades of yellow and orange. It hung loosely on her, ending mid-calf.

He realized it was probably the most modest outfit he'd seen her wear. Her hair was brushed and it was confined in a ponytail at the back of her neck. Her skin looked fresh and clean. Maybe she had on some mascara, but nothing else.

She also was acting pretty mad. "What's wrong with you?"

"Do you really need to ask?"

"You still upset about me accidentally hitting you?"

"Of course I am."

Remembering how out of control he'd been . . . and how guilty he'd felt, Calvin could hardly look her in the eye. "I already apologized for that."

"Not really. Not enough."

"Give me a break, Lora, wouldja? I won't be here long. I just needed someplace private to hang out for a couple of minutes."

Her gaze sharpened but she said nothing, only pulled out a glass and a pitcher of water from the refrigerator. "Want some?"

"Yeah. Sure."

She poured two glasses of water and handed him one as she sat down in the other chair at her small table. "Why are you really here?" she said after draining half the glass. "And don't tell me it's to rest and relax."

Calvin noticed that her eyes were averted. Her voice was thick, and she was acting far differently than she had the first time he'd shown up unannounced. Like night and day.

"What is wrong with you?" he asked. "You're acting as if you don't even know me. Like we've never been friends. Like you and I weren't hanging out together just last week."

Her eyes flashed. "Calvin, don't act like the trouble is with me. You hit me—then ran off."

"I'm here now."

"You sure are," she said sarcastically. "After serving food for seven hours at Bill's, I walk into my own house to find you sitting at this table. Looking like you don't have a care in the world. Of course I'm going to be surprised and ticked off."

He figured she had a point. But if he conceded that, he'd feel obligated to leave.

And then where would he go?

Therefore, he fastened on to the one thing she couldn't dispute. "What do you mean, working at Bill's?"

"I work at Bill's Diner. Did you not even know that?"

He hadn't. He hadn't really thought about it. "You a waitress there?"

She nodded. Lifting her chin, she said, "I've had this job fourteen months now."

She'd kept the same job for fourteen months. For over a year. It hit him then that she'd been obviously counting those months. She was proud of herself. "So that's why you're so dressed up."

She looked down at her sundress and shrugged. "Why are you here, Calvin? You never said."

Knowing that he had to come up with a topic before she threw him out, he said, "I talked to that sheriff. He said he and his deputy talked to you."

"Yeah. Sheriff Brewer and Deputy Beck came over to see me the morning after we sat here and got drunk together." She frowned. "This place was a mess. At first, I thought he was going to arrest me because the living room smelled like pot."

"He didn't?"

"No. He did look around, though."

"Did he have a search warrant?"

"I didn't care. It wasn't like he was going to find anything." Her expression tightened. "I was kind of out of it, Calvin. My face really hurt."

"What did you tell him about me?"

"That I had the beer but you had the pot."

Panic was setting in. "Is that it?"

Leaning up against one of those white counters, she sipped her water. "Yes," she said after a moment. "I mean no."

"Which is it?"

"I don't know."

"Lora, this is important. I'm afraid the sheriff wants to blame me for Amy Miller getting hurt." Then there was the whole drug thing. And maybe even his ties to the gang he owed so much money to.

"I don't know what you want me to say, Calvin. If you're asking if I told the sheriff or Deputy Beck that I thought you were trouble, I didn't." Looking at him coolly, she said, "But I didn't defend you, either."

"I thought we were friends."

After draining her glass of water, she turned on the tap and got some more. All while he stood there and fumed.

When she turned his way again, her expression was distant. Almost like she was stuck talking to a stranger. "Calvin, you and I have a past. We've also had some good times together. But that night we spent together was a mistake. You caught me at a weak moment."

"I didn't force you to do anything, Lora."

"I'm not saying you did. But I'm also not going to repeat it. Ever. I'm not like that any-more."

"You were the other day."

Looking incredulous, she said, "What do I have to say for you to understand how I'm feeling? I regret letting you in my house. I regret drinking with you. I regret smoking pot with you. I regret our argument. I regret that I wasn't strong enough to stop you from hitting me."

Needing to distance himself from her words, he leaned against the opposite row of cabinets. "You're being dramatic."

"Maybe I am. But what I am sayin' is that you are toxic, Calvin Fisher. You've come back here after ten years. A whole decade. And you have nothing to show for yourself except some scars marking your body and an attitude that is selfish and mean."

"I had to leave home at fourteen. Don't you know how hard that was?"

"Boo. Hoo," she taunted, sarcasm thick in her voice. "Like you're the only person in Hart County who has had bad stuff happen to them."

Memories that he fought so hard to forget bubbled up to the surface. Suddenly, he smelled the dirt and mildew in the house. Smelled the stale liquor, the unwashed dishes. The empty cabinets. Heard his father yelling at him. At all of them. "You don't know what the inside of my house was like."

"Sure I do. But even if I didn't, I do know what your brother is like."

"What is he like?" he asked harshly. "Perfect? Stuck-up? Far too full of himself?"

"Maybe he has moved on. Moved forward."

Jealousy hit him hard. "Is that who you're trying to impress, Lora? My older brother? Just like when we were in school and you used to sidle up next to him and try to get his attention?" Ignoring her look of embarrassment, he stood up, too. "Just to let you know, he ain't never going to give a person like you the time of day. He's got his eye on Waneta Cain, who's so pure and sweet, it's amazing she doesn't melt when it rains."

"You need to leave."

"Oh, don't act so hurt. You didn't really think that a girl like you would ever be good enough for my high and mighty brother, did you? Mark Fisher would never want a girl like you. Especially not when he finds out everything you've done over the years."

"I am not trying to snag your brother."

"Oh, is it someone else, then? Someone good? Someone other people respect?"

He knew he'd hit the mark when she visibly flinched. "Get out of here, Calvin. Get out before I call the sheriff and tell him that I'm afraid of you."

"Don't worry. I'm leaving," he said as he walked to her back door and yanked it open. "But I'm warning ya, Lora Weaver. If you start thinking that you can change, you're in for a real surprise. People like you and me won't ever change. And we're never going to be good enough for the likes of Mark Fisher or Waneta Cain. To them, you and I are always going to be worthless. Trash."

Pain filled her eyes. "That's not true."

"Of course it is. We might be older and we might even be smarter. But some things never change. Not for people like us," he said quietly as he started walking.

He picked up his pace when he heard her cry. Knew he'd just hurt her badly.

If Calvin wasn't feeling so much pain already, he knew he'd feel terrible.

But all he felt at the moment was numb.

Chapter 24

Tuesday, August 16

Only after Calvin disappeared from sight did Lora close the door. Then, because his words were still ringing in her ears, practically infecting her, she locked it and flipped the deadbolt for good measure.

She'd meant what she'd told him. He was toxic. His cruel comments and negative outlook infected her, made her doubt herself, made her doubt everything she tried to believe about herself.

Feeling sick, she downed another glass of water. One of her self-help books she'd been reading had advised doing that. Something about how water was cleansing. Lora wasn't all that sure if it was cleansing her insides or not, but she figured it was worth a try.

After all, she had plenty of water from the tap on hand.

Once she was calmer, she put Calvin's glass in the sink, then opened the two plastic sacks she'd set on the counter when she'd first seen Calvin in her kitchen.

One of the good things about working at Bill's was the fact that servers often got to take home leftovers. Today, she'd brought home a carton of beef stew, some macaroni and cheese, and two slices of cherry pie.

After setting the cardboard containers in the refrigerator, she picked up a rag to clean up her counters. But they were as white and pristine as she'd left them that morning. She sighed in relief.

Another one of her books had suggested doing home improvements every time she had a craving for doing something that she shouldn't. She'd taken that advice to heart. A year ago, she'd repainted the kitchen a pale turquoise. The cheery color had instantly made each day feel more optimistic.

After that, she'd bought some industrial-strength cleaner that Bill had recommended and scrubbed and scrubbed her countertops. Now they were a squeaky-clean white. It was silly, but she felt like they were a symbol for herself. Under all the grime and mistakes, there were some good things. She just had to work on uncovering them.

On her days off, she was tackling the tile in her bathroom. One day she hoped it would look as fresh as the countertops. She didn't know if it was possible, but she was going to try.

If only she could make Calvin's words vanish so easily!

Still feeling off-kilter, she walked to the bath-room and stood in front of the mirror. Looked at her skin—she still had lines around her lips from smoking for all those years, a scar on her arm from the car accident she'd been in.

The shadows under her eyes.

Even though she was in a new dress and her hair was shiny and clean, she still had a long way to go to be untarnished.

Maybe Calvin was right. Maybe she was an idiot, forever thinking she could change and that someone good and decent would think she was that way, too.

But just as she was about to turn away, she noticed something else. Her eyes were brighter. Her body was okay, too. She wasn't skinny and malnourished anymore. She looked healthy. Normal.

Why, if she didn't tell someone about all the things she'd done, they would probably never even guess.

She *was* better.

The phone rang. Running to her purse, she dug it out. Staring at the screen, she considered ignoring the call. What did the sheriff's office want from her now?

However, if she ignored it, then they would probably come find her again. She couldn't deal with another house call from them.

"Hello?" she said at last.

"Lora!" an unexpected voice said. "I was about to hang up. This is Eddie Beck. I'm glad you answered."

He was glad? She had no idea how to respond to that. "Hi, Deputy Beck," she said at last. "I, uh, was washing my hands. It took me a minute to grab the phone."

"Nothing to apologize for. And listen, I thought we had made it to first names by now. Haven't we?"

"Well, um . . ."

"My name is Eddie."

Oh, she knew. Now he was making her flustered. "I remembered." When he said nothing, she mumbled, "I mean, yes, we did make it to first names. Hello, Eddie." Great. Now she sounded like she was back in eighth grade. Her voice was sharp and she was fumbling over every word. "Um . . . did you need something?"

"I did." He paused, then blurted, "Sorry for the late notice, but is there any chance you are free right now?"

She gripped her cell phone a little tighter as despair settled into the pit of her stomach. What had happened now?

More importantly, why did the deputy think she had something to do with it?

Unless . . . it had something to do with Calvin? A handful of worst-case scenarios came to mind. Maybe he was watching her house? Maybe the deputy had just seen him leaving?

"Why? What's happened?"

"Nothing." He sounded taken aback.

"I don't understand, then."

"Well, you see, I've got the rest of the afternoon off. And, well, I don't know if you noticed, but for once it's not a hundred percent humidity. It's actually kind of bearable outside. Almost pleasant."

"It is nice."

"So, I wondered if you would like to go to Nolin Lake with me? There are some nice walking trails along the lake, and a great place for fried fish and burgers."

Her toes curled against the floor as the reason for his call sunk in. Deputy Eddie Beck wasn't calling to question her. Or to let her know that he saw Calvin walking out of her house.

He wasn't calling her for a business reason at all. No, it was personal.

Just to make sure she wasn't misunderstanding, she said tentatively, "Eddie, are you asking me out?"

He chuckled. "I guess I am, though I must be doing a really bad job of it if you have to ask."

"No, it is good. I was just surprised." She covered her phone with her palm and cleared her throat. Her voice sounded off. Hoarse.

"Surprised in a good way? Or bad?"

"In a good way," she replied, chuckling. "The best way."

"So is that a yes?" His voice was warm. Hopeful. "May I come pick you up in about a half hour? I promise, I'll be in my truck, not a police cruiser."

Feeling like she was in a daze, she nodded. Then remembered he was still waiting on the other end of the line. "Yes. A half hour is fine. I'll be ready. *Danke*." She shook her head. "I mean, thank you for the invitation."

"You're welcome, Lora. See you soon."

Only when she clicked off did she realize that Eddie had answered her in Pennsylvania Dutch, because she'd accepted in *Deutsch*!

Pressing her hands to her cheeks, she chuckled again.

And realized that Calvin couldn't have been more wrong. She could change. She could be more than she'd thought. She was worth it.

Even to people like Eddie Beck.

Lora was still feeling a lovely glow four hours later. She and Eddie had had a wonderful time. They'd walked along the shores of Nolin Lake, talking about sports, Eddie's basset hound, and her latest home improvement project.

They'd had fish-and-chips in a cute restaurant next to the docks. Then he'd kissed her on the cheek at her front door and waited until she got safely inside before going back to his vehicle. Just like a character in one of those romantic comedy movies she liked so much.

After she'd closed the door, Lora turned on the small light in the hall and then peeked out the window while he started his car and pulled away. For the first time in her life—that she could remember anyway—she felt content.

She felt normal and cared for and almost hopeful about the future.

"You have no shame, do you?"

Stifling a scream, Lora whirled around. When she saw him standing in the doorway of her kitchen, pure panic set in. "What are you doing here?"

"Not a lot. Only waiting. Waiting almost an hour." Even in the dim light, his expression looked full of disdain. "You should have been home, Lora."

"You need to leave," she said in a firm tone. "You can't just come in here and wait for me."

"I need to talk to you. But it's obvious that talking ain't going to help you change your ways, is it?"

She was shaking now. Ruthlessly, she fisted her hands, hoping the slight pinch of her nails digging into her palms would give her the control she needed to have.

He noticed. A triumphant gleam entered his expression. He was glad she was afraid.

"It's been you, hasn't it?" she whispered. "You are the man who attacked Amy Miller."

"Amy wasn't behaving right. She was lying to her parents. Dishonoring her family."

"You wore a mask with her." Her voice was trembling. To her amazement, she realized that there was still a small part of her that was waiting for him to deny her allegations. To tell her that it hadn't been him at all.

But instead, his voice turned hoarse. "I had no choice. She would've been able to identify me."

His voice was calm and even. As if they were talking about the menu at Bill's. As if he was in complete control of himself.

But she recognized that look in his eyes. It was the same one that had appeared in some of the men's faces when she'd walked into homeless shelters late at night. Whether it was from drugs, alcohol, or derived from pure anger and hate, she knew it was going to only bring her pain.

Especially since she was afraid he had a very good reason for not wearing a mask. He didn't plan for her to be alive to identify him one day.

She stepped back toward the door.

"Don't," he barked.

But Lora knew better than to believe that obeying him was going to help her. She stepped backward again. Then, turned and ran to the door and pulled open the handle. She had to get away from him.

Just as she stepped through the threshold, he grabbed her shoulders and threw her down to the ground. She screamed as her head hit the hard linoleum floor while her shoulders grazed the inside of the doorframe.

"You won't ever learn, will you, Lora?" he asked as he pulled her inside.

She fought. Kicking and twisting, she screamed again as her back slid along the cool floor. Screamed as loud as she could, for once thankful that she didn't live on an acre of property on the outskirts of town. Surely, someone would hear her.

"*Nee!*" With a grunt, he hit her hard. Hit her mouth.

She tasted blood as her lips tore against her teeth. Pain ebbed from the cut, radiated through her head, making her feel disoriented. But still she fought back. With as much power as she could, she pushed at his shoulders.

He grunted before hitting her again. This time harder. Spots filled her vision, and she knew she was about to black out. But she'd been through far too much to simply give up. Since her body was weakening, she had to use the only thing left to her.

Her voice.

"You can't keep hurting women like this. You are going to be discovered. Then punished."

"By whom? Your police officer?" His voice was filled with sarcasm as he shifted to slam the door shut.

Effectively ending her effort to get away.

Dark acceptance filled her. She wasn't going to be able to run away. Or fight back. Or stop whatever he was about to do. Her body was hurting too much, her head was pounding too hard.

Therefore she glared at her attacker, letting all the disdain she felt for him seep into her expression. "You aren't going to get anything right, are you?" she whispered. "Eddie Beck ain't a policeman. He's a sheriff's deputy. And oh, yes, he will punish you for this. Of that I have no doubt."

Then all her words left as he grabbed her shoulders, shook her hard, then hit her again. And several more times after that.

Chapter 25

"Mark, you don't need to start walking me to work. I'll be fine," Waneta said as they started down her driveway.

"Like I told you the other day, you mean something to me. Something important. I'm not going to take a risk with your safety."

Her heart melted. Mark made her feel feminine and protected. She knew she shouldn't yearn for such things, that she should want to feel independent and self-assured, but the last year had taken its toll. She'd been spending her life on autopilot, dutifully going from her duties at work to tackling her chores at home.

She'd known she'd been tired. She'd known she'd been emotionally exhausted, but she hadn't realized how drained she'd been. Mark's attentions and protective nature made her feel a little weak. More than a little warm and mushy inside.

She wasn't sure why God had decided that now was their time together, but she couldn't deny that His timing had been impeccable. Just when she'd needed someone the most, Mark had arrived in her life.

But that didn't mean she wanted to take advantage of his goodness.

"I could have ridden my bike, you know. If I thought I was in danger, I could simply pedal faster."

"You think a blue bicycle with a brown wicker basket is going to save you from someone trying to do you harm?"

"Maybe. Especially since I don't think I'm going to come to any harm."

"Since I don't want to hurt your feelings, I won't mention Amy Miller, then."

"Well, that's a sneaky way of adding your two cents," she said, though his comment *had* hit its mark. She was still shaken up by Amy's attack.

"I'm going to do whatever I can to make you take your safety seriously," he said as he moved her closer to the side of the road as a vehicle approached. "You mean too much to me to keep my feelings to myself."

As it slowed and veered around them, Waneta noticed that the driver had waved at them as he passed. No doubt he was thinking they were a sweet Amish couple walking together.

And maybe that's what they were. She had on a light-green dress with short sleeves, a white *kapp*, and rubber flip-flops. Next to her, Mark was in brighter colors, wearing a short-sleeved bright-blue shirt and black pants, set off by his straw hat. He was also carrying her lunch cooler.

"I feel a little like we're on our way to school and you're carrying my lunch," she teased.

"We're pretty close to that." Smiling, he said, "But that would have been nice, don't you think?"

"If we were younger and still in school?"

"If we could go back in time and take advantage of the opportunities the Lord gave us. If I had been smarter, I could have courted you then. It would have saved me a lot of trouble."

She supposed he had a point. But as wonderful as it sounded now, she doubted she would have been in the right frame of mind back then to have been his sweetheart. She'd been too sheltered and tentative about anything that was different than the narrow world she knew.

And Mark? Well, she didn't remember him acting this way. He'd been restless and angry. Now, of course, she knew why. Back then? . . .

She hadn't really wanted to know.

"I think we were meant to wait for each other," she said softly. "Though it would have saved us some hardships, I don't know if it would have saved us from a bunch of other problems."

A muscle in his cheek twitched before he nodded. "You know, I think you are probably right. This is our time. And because of everything we've been through—not in spite of it—I know we are meant to be together."

Now her insides felt like jelly. Mark really did say the sweetest things. "Just for that, I'm going to let you share my lunch."

He bent his elbow, pretending to groan, as if her cooler weighed a hundred pounds. "I hope so, because if you intended to eat all this food, I'd be mighty worried about you."

"Are you sure you can carry that cooler without a problem? Your hand is awfully bruised."

"Oh, it's nothing. I just knocked it wrong when I was attempting to repair some old woodwork."

"It's more than nothing. It's mighty swollen."

He shrugged. "I'll survive. Or maybe Henry will feel sorry for me and make you do all the heavy lifting today."

"I'm stronger than I look. You forget that I did your job for years before you arrived."

"I haven't forgotten. You do like to boss me around."

She was giggling as he moved her to the shoulder of the road again.

"Careful, now," he murmured. "Some of these cars go by far too fast."

As the vehicle approached, Mark tensed. "This one don't seem— *Ah,* it's the sheriff."

Waneta stopped as they watched Sheriff Brewer's vehicle slow down beside them. The passenger-side window rolled down, revealing Deputy Beck.

"Morning," he said. "We were on our way to Blooms and Berries to speak to you."

"To me?" Waneta asked curiously . . . just seconds before panic set in. "Oh, no! Did something happen to my *daed*?"

After the vehicle stopped, the deputy got out. "Your parents are fine, Neeta," he soothed.

"Then what do you need?"

Sheriff Brewer's door opened and shut. "We were looking for Mark, not you."

Mark stepped closer to her. She wondered if he was trying to ease her concerns or allay his own. "What happened?" he asked.

"The side of the road isn't the best place to have this discussion," the deputy said. "We'd like to take you in."

"To the station?" Mark's expression turned stormy. "I think you need to explain yourselves right here first."

"Lora Weaver was attacked last night," Sheriff Brewer said.

"She almost died," the deputy added. "She wasn't found until this morning when she didn't show up for work and her boss got concerned."

"Who found her?" Mark asked.

The deputy glared at him. "I did. She was lying on the floor, barely breathing. Blood all around her. It's amazing she is still alive."

Imagining poor Lora, Waneta started shaking.

Mark curved his arm protectively around her. "Careful, now," he warned the officers. "There's a better way to tell a woman news like this. Bluntly on the side of the road ain't it."

"This was the way you wanted to handle it, though," Deputy Beck said. "As if you really cared."

Mark's expression turned to stone. "What are you saying?"

Before either of the officers could reply, Waneta raised her voice. "Who could have done this? Is Lora going to be all right?"

"The ambulance took her in. I sent a man out to fetch her sister," Sheriff Brewer said. "But she's unconscious. They're running some tests now to check for bleeding."

"So you don't know who did it?"

"We have some ideas," the deputy said quietly as he reached for his arm. "Now, it's time you came with us."

Mark jerked his arm away. "I had nothing to do with Lora getting hurt. I was friends with her."

"That wasn't what she said."

"When?" Mark said, his voice incredulous. "You just told us that she wasn't awake."

Ignoring Mark's retort, Deputy Beck shot off another question. "What were you doing last night?"

"I was working in my house."

"Alone?"

"Yes. Of course."

"How did you get that bruise and scrape on your hand?"

Staring at his hand, Mark flexed his fingers. "I was repairing some corner woodwork," he said slowly. "Wait. You really do suspect me, don't you?"

Sheriff Brewer stepped closer. "As much as it pains me to do this, I need you to come to the station with me, son."

Mark shook his head. "I told you I'd never allow you to put me through that again. I had nothing to do with Lora getting hurt."

Deputy Beck gripped his arm. "You can either get in the vehicle without arguing or we can slip some handcuffs on you."

Waneta shook her head. "*Nee*! Sheriff Brewer, don't do this."

"Deputy Beck is going to walk you back home, Waneta."

"*Nee*." Feeling frantic now, she rushed toward Mark. "I don't know what to do. How can I help?"

Pain filled his expression as he gazed at her. "Calm down, Waneta. I'll be all right."

"*Nee*, you aren't—"

"I promise, I'll be fine. See? I'm getting in the car now," he continued easily. "Go on home now."

"Mark, I canna just stand here and do nothing."

Looking even more grim, he said, "You won't. You'll be staying safe, which is more important. Go home, Neeta. I'll come over when I'm done."

Waneta stood helplessly as she watched Sheriff Brewer open the back passenger door and guide Mark in, then get in the driver's seat.

She was frozen as she stood by the deputy's side while the car pulled out and drove toward town.

"Is this yours?" Deputy Beck picked up the heavy cooler.

Seeing that cooler was the tipping point. Because it wasn't really hers. That food was for Mark and her to share. There was no way she was going to be able to enjoy it without him beside her.

Tears filled her eyes. "*Jah.*"

"Waneta, we have a couple of choices," he said quietly. "I can walk you back home or I can call and have someone pick us up."

All she could seem to do was stare at him. Lora was unconscious. Mark had been taken in for questioning. None of it felt real.

He cleared his throat. "I'm sorry. I'm sure you are having a difficult time, but I need your help. I need to get to the hospital as soon as I can."

She didn't want to walk anywhere with him.

How could he have thought Mark would hurt Lora? But standing on the side of the road wasn't an option.

"I don't want to go home. I'd rather go to work."

"Are you sure?"

"*Nee*. But, as you said, you need an answer. I gave you one."

A muscle in his cheek jumped. "Understood. Let's start walking, then."

She picked up her tote and began leading the way. She was hardly able to look at him, she felt so betrayed. Luckily, she and Mark had been almost halfway there when Sheriff Brewer and Deputy Beck stopped beside them.

If the deputy was upset about her silence, he didn't let on. He simply kept looking straight ahead and matched his pace with hers.

When Blooms and Berries came into sight, her anger bubbled over. "Mark would never hurt Lora."

"He's only being taken in for questioning."

"When Sheriff Brewer questions him, he'll realize that Mark is innocent."

"Someone beat Lora Weaver badly. They need to pay for that."

Hating his tone, she whirled around to glare at him. "Is that what you are going to do at the hospital, then? Stand vigil by her bedside until she can give you a name?"

His light-green eyes looked like shards of ice. "I am going to sit by Lora's bedside because I can't bear the thought of her waking alone."

"You care about her—"

"Of course I care," he snapped. "Lora was beaten. She could slip into a coma. She could wake up and be blind." After a pause, he added, "The question is, don't you care, too?"

The force of his tone, together with his devastated expression, gave her pause. "Of course I care. I've known Lora for years."

"Did you really know her? Or did you just know of her?"

She heard something new in his tone. Almost like he was chastising her. "What is that supposed to mean?"

"It means that she was pretty alone here in this town. Every time I saw her, she was either working or home alone. She only mentioned having work friends. Or, maybe you just judged her on how she looked and on her past."

"If I did those things, I didn't do it intentionally."

He raised his eyebrows. "You sure about that?"

"*Jah.*" At least, she thought she was. "If I have harmed her feelings in some way, I'll do my best to apologize. I'll make amends."

"I see."

His voice had an edge of sarcasm to it. She didn't know where his antagonism toward her came from, but she didn't appreciate it. Not under the latest circumstances.

Feeling hurt and worried and more than a little irritated with him and Sheriff Brewer, Waneta grabbed her cooler.

"Do you hear what I'm saying, Deputy Beck? I hope so, since I'm currently of the mind that you and Sheriff Brewer might be doing the very same thing with Mark Fisher." While he gaped at her, she said, "My place of work is right here. I'll see myself there now."

After turning, she rushed to the entrance.

When she got there, Henry Lehmann looked up from a garden supply magazine he was studying. "Waneta? What's wrong? Where's Mark?"

Finally, there in the safety of the store, she rushed to her boss's side and burst into tears.

Chapter 26

Wednesday, August 17

The room Mark was in was all too familiar. Beige walls. Faded yellow, scratched linoleum tile on the floor. Three chairs made out of particle wood surrounding a metal table with an avocado-green vinyl top that was nicked and torn. The room smelled like he remembered, too. Vaguely of disinfectant and dirty shoes, with a good dose of sweat and starch mixed in.

As Mark shifted in his chair across from Sheriff Brewer, he figured that it was probably just as well that the environment was so familiar, since the participants were the same. After all, it had been just a little over two years ago when he'd sat in this very same place for almost the very same reason.

But instead of feeling scared to death and sure that Sheriff Brewer and the rest of Hart County, Kentucky, was out to get him, this time Mark only felt irritated with the situation.

And impatient.

He was impatient that their "meeting" was taking so long. He needed to get out of the room and check on Waneta. He hated that she was at home fretting about him.

He also felt a deep sadness for Lora. He hoped and prayed that she would recover.

Across from him, Sheriff Brewer also seemed different. The last time he'd questioned Mark, he'd been intent, focused, and transparently sure of Mark's guilt. However, so far, he'd been rather apologetic. Almost as if he hadn't wanted to pick Mark up in the first place but hadn't had much of a choice.

Now he was sipping coffee and staring at a blank pad of paper. His left hand was playing with a pencil, twirling it between two fingers.

Mark wasn't sure why the silence had gone on so long, but he was getting bored with it. "You're left-handed?" he asked, just because the silence was getting to him.

Sheriff Brewer looked down at his hand, then stared at Mark in surprise. "Yeah. I am. Why?"

"No reason. I am, too."

Brewer dropped the pencil. "Used to be, lefties were a rarity. Now there are quite a few of us."

"I've noticed that, too. Even among the Amish."

"Still hard to find a pair of left-handed scissors, though." The sheriff flashed a smile before shifting in his chair. While the cheap material creaked and groaned beneath him, he seemed to get back on track. "We need to go back to what you were doing last night. You say you were working on your house's woodwork?"

"Yes."

"Now, why were you doing that again?"

"It shouldn't be that big of a surprise. You've seen my house. What my father didn't neglect or ruin, four months sitting vacant did."

"Tell me how, exactly, you bruised your hand." As if he could tell that Mark was about to point out that they'd already discussed this in length, Sheriff Brewer raised his eyebrows. "Again, if you please."

"I hurt my knuckles refitting warped woodwork. I had a crowbar in one hand and was trying to pop the wood into the space. My hand slipped, and the crowbar bumped it."

"Bet that hurt."

It had, but it surely wasn't anything to complain about. Pressing his hands flat on the vinyl tabletop, Mark leaned slightly forward. "Sheriff, I ain't some naïve Amish man with a chip on my shoulder anymore. I know about evidence and fingerprints and DNA testing. I know you've already combed poor Lora's house for samples and maybe even checked her fingernails while she lay unconscious. You ain't going to find anything from me. I haven't been in her house and I haven't touched her."

"But what about Calvin?"

He inhaled sharply.

Sheriff Brewer had hit his target, Mark would give him that. He felt as if someone had kicked him in the chest, then decided to rest his boot there awhile. As he tried to regain his composure, the sheriff looked unperturbed.

He actually kicked his legs out in front of him, crossed his ankles, and took a sip of coffee.

"I canna answer for my brother," Mark said at last.

"Why not?"

"I haven't seen him in days."

"What day, exactly, did you see him last?"

Mark tried to recall the day. Was it last Tuesday? Friday? "Maybe Thursday or Friday of last week? I can't really remember."

"Why not? I would remember the last time I saw my brother."

"Perhaps your brother is the type of man you look forward to seeing. Mine is not." Before the officer could ask some inane question about why, Mark stared hard at him. "And we know why, too," he said. "Calvin is running with a bad crowd and is making poor decisions. I gave up parenting him when he ran away years ago."

"I've done some checking on him. A couple of informants from Louisville say he owes folks some money."

"Then he probably does." This was news to him, but not surprising.

"He hit Lora the other night. She told us that."

"I know."

"So . . ."

"I don't know what happened, Sheriff Brewer. I don't know what happened between Calvin and Lora at her house. I don't know what happened to Amy in her front yard. I don't know who attacked Lora in her house." Taking a deep breath, he let his frustration show. "All I do know is that I worked on my house last night and had the privilege of walking Waneta Cain to work this morning, when you and your deputy plucked me off the street. Waneta is no doubt scared, Henry is no doubt lifting too much at work, and Lora is in the hospital. I need to get out of here and be of use."

"You seem different now, Mark," the sheriff said slowly.

"That's because I am different. I'm better."

Sheriff Brewer stood up. "Can I give you a ride home?"

Mark knew it was as close to an apology as he was going to get for being questioned that morning.

With a burst of awareness, Mark realized he didn't actually need one. He was becoming confident enough not to need reassurance from everyone he knew to feel good about himself.

Maybe he really had come a long way.

"You can give me a ride to Blooms and Berries," he said with a smile. "I need to make sure Henry ain't overexerting himself."

Sheriff Brewer smiled. "Let's go, then."

When Mark got out of the sheriff's vehicle, he wasn't sure what to expect. He doubted Henry Lehmann was going to treat him any differently, but he was the only person he felt sure about.

As for everyone else? Well, he knew some would look at him as the most obvious suspect in Lora's attack. He was prepared to deal with that. But if his getting picked up for questioning had ruined everything between him and Waneta, it was going to crush him. He knew now that he didn't just care for her. He didn't just like her, either.

He'd fallen in love with her. He held her in the highest regard, and he would be devastated if she didn't trust him anymore.

To his surprise, the shop was crowded. Mark didn't know why he was so surprised. It just felt strange that the rest of the world continued on while his own felt like it was lying on its side.

Mostly English customers were roaming the aisles. Some he recognized, a few he knew well enough to shake hands with and say hello. Waneta and Henry were behind the counter, working side by side. Ben was nearby, stocking and assisting.

Mark breathed a sigh of relief. He was really glad someone was helping them with the heavy lifting in the heat.

When he approached, Henry raised his head. "Mark. Good day."

Waneta was running a credit card and wrapping up a woman's purchases. Mark supposed that was the reason she hadn't turned to smile at him.

But his boss's expression looked carefully blank as well.

Mark's stomach sank. Could he not even trust Henry to believe in him?

"Good day," he replied softly. "I'm sorry I'm late."

"I expect you had good reason."

"I'm ready now. Where would you like me?"

"Go to the storeroom, wouldja? There's a new apron for you there."

Mark raised his eyebrows but did as he was bid. He really hoped that Henry wasn't trying to get him out of sight.

When he opened the storeroom, though, he literally gasped.

His brother, Calvin, was sitting on an upturned bucket, sorting seed packets.

"Hey," he said. "I had just about given up on you."

"Calvin." Feeling stunned, he stumbled over his words. "Does Henry know you're here?"

278

"Of course. I wouldn't be sorting seeds on my own."

That was Calvin. Ready with a flippant reply that hid the seriousness of the situation. Actually, he spoke like his showing up at Blooms and Berries made perfect sense.

It didn't.

As Mark thought about Lora's injuries, Waneta's friendship, Sheriff Brewer questioning him, then driving him here, he realized that Calvin's appearance in the storage room fit right in with how everything in their lives was going.

Nothing made perfect sense at the moment.

Chapter 27

Wednesday, August 17

"W hat are you doing here?" Mark asked. Eyeing his brother, Calvin relaxed. Mark wasn't yelling at him or telling him to get out of his life. It was a small thing, but an improvement. "I heard about Lora . . . and that you were taken in for questioning. I figured you might need a hand."

In a move out of their childhood, Mark visibly got control of himself. After a few seconds, Calvin strode closer. "I've been worried about you. Where have you been?"

Wasn't that how it had always been? Even when he was in so much hot water that he could barely breathe, his brother still concentrated on him.

If he hadn't thought Mark would have taken it the wrong way, Calvin would have laughed. Instead, he got to his feet. They were the same height. Roughly the same build. Calvin hoped that would remind his brother that he wasn't a weakling needing to be looked after. "Where do you think I've been?"

"I couldn't even begin to imagine."

Huh. It seemed Mark wasn't attempting to act calm and nurturing after all. "You sound as if you've been imagining a lot of things, actually. What have you been picturing me doing, Mark? Maybe that I took myself over to Lora's *haus* last night and decided to beat her bloody?"

Mark's neck flushed, giving Calvin his answer. "You hit her before."

It was hard, but Calvin stayed steady. "You're right. I did. I hit her and apologized for it. It don't help that I was drunk and stoned, does it?"

"*Nee.* That was no excuse."

"You're right. It don't matter at all. I got mad, did something I was ashamed of, and hurt her in the process."

Mark just stared, his expression cool. "I still don't know where you've been."

"Because you don't need to know. But we do need to talk. That's why I'm here. Because we need to talk about some things."

"Actually, well, now ain't the best—"

"I get it, Mark," Calvin interrupted. "I get that you are never going to want to hear what I have to say."

"Hold on. I didn't say that."

But his pensive expression told Calvin otherwise. "We have a lifetime of hurts and mistakes that lie between us like a deep, dark pool. We are afraid to get closer because we don't know what we're going to find between us. Maybe we're afraid of drowning."

"I never thought you were the type of man to bring up metaphors."

Calvin smiled. "Really? Did you ever pay attention to what I could do, Mark?" he asked softly. "Or was it easier to simply concentrate on what I couldn't do. What I didn't do."

"Don't make our childhood into something it wasn't. Of course I was never your buddy or your pal. I grew up having to take care of you."

"And I grew up knowing that you had to. How do you think that felt?"

Mark swallowed. "What does it matter? You're an adult now."

Choosing his words with care, he said, "It matters because I was your burden. When I left, I knew you weren't going to understand why."

"I know you got into a lot of trouble. I know you left me alone to take care of our father."

Calvin flinched. He'd conveniently given himself a dozen excuses and reasons that justified his leaving. More food for Mark. Less tension in the house. Mark could have more time for himself. Never had he thought that his brother had felt much more than relief at his departure.

"We might have too much between us to ever get along. But I need you to put our pasts behind us for a little while and give me a few minutes of your time." When Mark looked like he was about to push him off again, Calvin added quickly, "Call it giving me just a smidge of the Lord's grace."

"Don't speak of the Lord."

"How about you stop acting so high and mighty?"

Mark pressed his palms to his face. Then, looking weary, he sat down on the edge of a stack of wooden crates. "What do you want to talk about?"

"I came to Horse Cave to find you because I heard you got the house. I wanted to convince you to sell it and give me half the money."

"I know. I haven't changed my mind. I'm not going to sell the house."

"Yeah, I figured that out. You don't think I deserve it."

Mark folded his arms across his chest. "Maybe I thought about that at first. But, really, the house needs so much work, I don't know how much money we would ever get for it. Or when it would sell. Then I would be back where I was—homeless. I can't live that way again."

Yet again, Mark's practical nature shamed him.

Or, maybe it was Lora getting hurt.

Until now, all Calvin had been thinking about was freeing himself from the gang. He hadn't considered all the consequences of his actions. Yet again. "I guess you're right," he said at last.

"Are you in a lot of trouble?"

"In trouble with the people I owe money to? Yeah. Some." Of course, that was a lie. He was in *a lot* of trouble, and out of ideas. There was a real good chance the gang wasn't going to let him live another two weeks unless a miracle happened.

"I don't have any extra funds to give you," Mark said. "Do you want to live back at home with me?"

He'd never imagined Mark would offer that. If Calvin wasn't so used to steeling himself against pain, he swore he would have started crying. He'd thought he'd lost everything.

"Thanks, but that place is never going to hold anything but bad memories for me."

Disappointment flickered in Mark's eyes before he steeled himself again. "So, is that what you wanted to tell me? That you came back here because you're in trouble?"

"Yeah. I mean, ain't that enough?"

Staring at him, Mark shook his head. "*Nee.*"

"I don't know what else you want from me."

"Maybe I want you to listen to me for a change."

"And hear what?"

"That I'm sorry. I shouldn't have pretended not to see you when you first showed up. I

284

shouldn't have acted like you were going to taint my relationship with Waneta." Looking exhausted, Mark sat down on a crate. "I guess I haven't changed all that much, after all. When we were young, I felt that I could never let my guard down. If I did, we'd get in trouble, or we wouldn't have any food. Or someone would want to try to separate us."

"You aren't wrong. You couldn't let your guard down. Our parents? Well, they weren't much good at parenting."

"They weren't much good at much," Mark corrected. "Anyway, lately, I've been trying so hard to rebuild my life that I had forgotten that I had to repair my past in order to do that. I should have put you first."

"I didn't come here to hear that."

"I'm glad you did, though." Optimism filled his tone. "Calvin, it's not too late. We can do that now. I want us to try to get to know each other again."

Calvin doubted he was going to live long enough for that to be possible, but he was willing to give it a try. "I want that, too," he said quietly.

When the storage room door opened, Henry Lehmann and Waneta Cain walked in.

Mark fairly jumped to his feet. "Waneta, hi," he said in a soft tone. "Are you all right?"

Crossing the room, she reached for his hands.

"I am now," she said with a bright, blinding smile. "We just heard that Lora is awake!"

"Praise the Lord," Henry said. "The doctors think she is going to make a full recovery."

"That's wonderful news. The best," Mark said, smiling right back at her.

"We also heard some news, though this was a bit harder to hear," Mr. Lehmann said. "Lora told the deputy who her attacker was."

"Who?" Mark asked.

"James Eicher."

Waneta inhaled sharply while Mark pressed his lips together. "Have they picked him up yet?" Mark asked.

Mr. Lehmann shook his head. "I don't believe so. I was mostly concerned with Lora, though."

Waneta gazed up at Mark. "I'd like to see her. I don't want her to think she's all alone."

"I thought you'd want to get over there," Mr. Lehmann said. "I just called for a driver to take you and Mark to the hospital. He should be here within ten minutes or so."

Calvin cleared his throat. "Can I go, too?" Realizing he sounded like a little kid, he shook his head in dismay. "I meant, well, I'd like to join you."

Mark smiled. "If you want to join us, we'd be happy to have you come along."

"I want to."

Waneta turned to him and smiled. "Everything is going to be so much better now. I'm sure of it."

Calvin didn't speak, but he did glance at Mark. Relief shone in his eyes.

It was the same exact way Calvin was feeling.

Lora was surprised to discover that Eddie Beck was still sitting at her bedside when she woke up from another long nap late that afternoon.

"You came back," she murmured, her voice thick with sleep.

"I did. After I went back to the office for a couple of hours, I told the sheriff that I wanted to come keep you company."

"That's sweet of you."

Taking her hand, he ran his thumb along her knuckles. "I didn't want you to be alone."

"I'm glad you're here."

He smiled, but the warmth didn't quite reach his eyes. He was worried. No doubt he was hoping for more information about James's attack. "Do you want me to talk about what happened now?"

"Do you mind? I know we already went through this once. Do you think you can handle telling me about the experience again?"

"Well, I can try. I mean, that's why you're here, right?"

Standing up, he leaned over and brushed a chunk of her hair away from her face. "Actually, no. I came back because I care about you, Lora. You are what is important to me."

He was so kind. He sounded so sincere. Her pulse quickened as she imagined them together. Then, just as quickly, she reminded herself that she was no doubt putting too much into his words. Why, he probably thought he should care about every person who lived in Hart County.

His eyes brightened. "Lora Weaver, never decide to start playing professional poker. I can read just about everything you are thinking."

"Even now?" she tried to joke. Her face was swollen and one of her eyes was almost shut.

"Especially now," he said as he brushed his hand through her hair again. "I'm not going to make you answer a bunch of questions or play games with you. I just want you to know that I'm here for one reason only. Because I want to be with you."

His words were so sweet. Soon, she knew she would treasure every word of their conversations, too.

But for now? She was too weak to do much except tell him what he needed to know. "Like I told you before, James was waiting for me when I got home from our date."

Pulling out his notebook, he flipped it open and started writing. "Tell me again what he was wearing. And what you remember him saying."

"It might take me a while," she warned. "I keep remembering everything out of order."

Pressing his lips to her brow, he whispered, "Take all the time you need. We'll talk about James, then we'll put it behind you and talk about something else."

"Such as?"

He chuckled. "Maybe I'll tell you a story or two, Lora."

Relaxing again, she started to talk. The words came easier now, maybe because she knew that their conversation wasn't about to end.

Like their relationship, it was only just beginning.

"You sure about this?" Mark asked when they stopped in front of Lora's house two days later.

"Mighty sure," Waneta said. "When I told Lora that I wanted to be a better friend to her, I meant what I said."

Taking her hand, he squeezed it. "I know that. I just don't want you to walk home from her house by yourself."

"I'm going to go straight home, Mark. I'll be careful." Releasing his hand, she gave him a little push. "Now, off you go. You have supper plans with Eli."

He smiled. "We're going out for Mexican. Turns out he likes spicy food as much as I do."

"Enjoy yourselves. Now, I've gotta go."

After he gave her a hug, she raced up Lora's walk and rapped on the door. After a minute or two, Lora opened the door.

"Boy, Mark sure doesn't like telling you good-bye," she teased.

Waneta smiled. "He's sweet . . . but I think he's actually more worried about me walking home alone. I told him I'd be fine, though."

"He has good reason," Lora said as she slowly made her way into the small living room. "But don't you worry. Eddie is going to stop by in an hour. He can walk you home."

"*Danke.*" Watching as Lora curled up in her chair, her penguin pajama bottoms and worn T-shirt making her look like a teenager, Waneta said, "How are you feeling?"

"A little better. One of my sisters came over last night. She helped me take a shower."

Though she was still bruised, Lora seemed to be getting around better. "I think the swelling might have gone down a little bit."

"I think it has, too." Pointing to a stack of frozen vegetable bags, Lora said, "Who knew frozen peas and carrots would feel so good?"

"They are lifesavers. My *mamm* swears by them," Waneta added. "Now, how about something to drink? I can make you some tea. Or maybe something cold?"

Lora raised an eyebrow. "You're not going to let me do a thing, are you?"

Already on her feet, Waneta shook her head. "Nope. I'm going to pick things up, do some dishes, and wait on you as much as you'll let me."

"I can't let you do that."

"Sure you can," Waneta called out from the kitchen. "Because I want something in return."

"What's that?"

Hearing the note of worry in Lora's voice, Waneta walked back to her side. "I want to know all about you and that deputy," she said.

This time it was Lora who was smiling kind of awkwardly. "I like him a lot."

"I can't wait to hear all about how you two met."

"Does that mean I can ask about you and Mark?"

Waneta nodded. "*Jah*. Because we're friends now. I mean, if you want to be."

"I do," Lora said.

After sharing another smile, Waneta hurried back to finish making them both tall glasses of iced tea.

In no time, James would be caught and everything would get back to normal. God had given her a warm and solid relationship with Mark and a new friendship with Lora.

Surely, He wouldn't do such things unless He intended for things to settle down in Hart County.

At least, she hoped that was the case.

Chapter 28

Three weeks had passed since Lora Weaver had identified James Eicher as her attacker. When Sheriff Brewer and Deputy Beck went to his house to arrest him for assaulting Lora Weaver, they'd discovered his wife Katie bruised and battered on their floor.

James was still nowhere to be found.

Katie later said that the moment James had heard that Lora had regained consciousness, he'd burst into a terrible rage.

That was the first time she had realized what James had been doing. When she'd tried to stop him from running out the door, he'd beaten her.

No one had any real idea where James could be. Everyone in the county seemed to have a guess—yet some people were sure that James would be hiding in Horse Cave, in one of the narrow, needle-like branches of the cavern under the town.

Waneta figured James hiding in a cave was as good a guess as any. After all, the cavern was only about fifty percent explored. There were too many dark and unstable areas that were prone to either flooding or at risk for caving in.

At first she and most other women in the area were on pins and needles, sure James was going to pop out of the cave's entrance and seek vengeance on them all.

But that hadn't happened.

Actually, as the days passed and inched toward September, very little did happen, with the exception of Waneta growing closer to Mark and Calvin showing up every so often, sometimes even staying the night with his brother. Things were still awkward between them, but at least they were communicating and trying to patch things up. That was something, she supposed.

After practically shadowing Waneta everywhere for weeks, Mark had finally begun to give her more space. She was thrilled. She loved spending time with him, but she'd begun to feel a little claustrophobic.

She usually enjoyed riding her bike or walking by herself sometimes. But her parents had insisted she take her bike to and from work. Her father pointed out that it was a little safer. She was happy to do that, and had already ridden it two times that week.

Riding made her feel like things were back to normal again. This morning, she'd even taken a longer route than usual, enjoying the morning air against her face as she navigated the hills and windy roads around Blooms and Berries.

But now that she was about to leave work, she realized she had a big problem.

It was still in the place where she'd parked it, but both tires were flat as pancakes. How had it managed to accrue not one but two flat tires?

Walking to her side, Mr. Lehmann gazed at the wheels with an expression that would have been funny if Waneta hadn't been so despondent. He was a man who enjoyed getting around on his feet or by horse. He didn't hold a lot of appreciation for bicycles.

"Neeta, what do you want to do with this contraption? Wheel it home?"

She understood his tone. It had been a long day. Really long. Customers had come in sporadically and when they did, they all seemed to be upset by something. By eleven o'clock, Waneta had felt like she did not have another ounce of patience left for argumentative, hard-to-please customers.

Thinking she needed her long day to be over, she said, "Mr. Lehmann, could we put my bike inside for tonight?"

"For sure. But how will you get home?"

"I'll walk."

"I thought your parents didn't want you walking no more."

"They don't, but it can't be helped. Besides,

before I got my bike, I walked here every day. I'm not about to call a driver to come get me."

"Of course not. Well, I'll lock this inside the storeroom and we'll figure out how to patch up the tires in the morning. Now, you should hurry home and get some rest. Tomorrow is sure to be a better day."

"I hope so. It couldn't get much worse."

He playfully shook a finger at her. "Don't say such things, girl. You're liable to jinx yourself."

Smiling at his joke, she grabbed her tote and cooler and trudged home.

By the end of the first mile, she was getting tired. Maybe she should have gotten a driver after all? It was hot and humid, making each step feel exhausting.

Then there were her nerves. They seemed to be getting the best of her. Though it was still daylight, hardly anyone was around. She kept imagining someone was watching her, which was ridiculous.

Increasing her pace, Waneta kept walking. Sweat ran down her neck, making the fabric of her dress stick to her skin. When she began breathing heavily, she forced herself to stop. The last thing she needed was to get overheated. Releasing her heavy cooler, she pulled at the fabric of her dress.

Attempted to fan herself.

But it didn't do much good.

She was nervous and hot. Tired and imagining things. Why, even the sound of a twig snapping behind her made her nerves on edge! Just to prove herself wrong, she glanced behind her when she picked up her cooler again.

And saw James Eicher standing right there.

"James?" she sputtered. "What are you doing here? Have you been following me?"

At first, he seemed surprised to hear her address him. But then he glared at her. "Don't speak."

He needn't have worried. Waneta didn't think she could form another word if she tried. He looked as angry as ever. With a shiver, she wondered if he'd worn the same expression when he'd attacked the other girls.

She needed to do something. Her only option was to run. Tossing her cooler at him, she turned and started running as fast as she could. Dirt kicked up under her flip-flops as the rubber soles slipped and slid against the packed earth.

Before she could pick up her pace, a hand dug into her shoulder. Pulled her back. Hard.

"Don't turn away from me."

She twisted her head to meet his gaze as his fingers pressed deeper into the soft area right above her collarbone. "Stop, James. You are hurting me."

"You need to learn to listen, Waneta."

Eyeing him closely, she knew she had to act fast. He was strong. She hadn't been able to outrun him. Her only option was to keep him talking until someone saw them. "Who do I need to listen to, James? You?"

Fire lit his eyes as he visibly struggled for control.

Attempting to pull her shoulder from his grasp, she said, "You need to go home. Leave me be. Accosting women on the street ain't good. The sheriff has been looking for you, you know."

Without warning, he slapped her hard.

She reeled back. Just as she was on the verge of losing her balance, he pulled her toward him, his grip on her upper arms now. They dug into her skin, his nails cutting her, stinging. Leaving her no choice but to bend to his wishes.

Looking into his eyes, Waneta realized that though he was angry at her, his eyes looked clear and calm. He knew exactly what he was doing. He'd planned for this.

Still holding her close, he spoke. "You were perfect. You were everything a proper woman should be. But then you ruined yourself. You became tainted."

She shook her head.

"You've accepted men into your life whom you shouldn't have even looked at. He ruined you."

"You're upset with me for being friends with Mark? After everything you've done, you are casting stones?" she asked, not even trying to hide the disdain in her voice. "You are being ridiculous."

"Don't speak to me like that."

"I wouldn't be talking to you at all if I could help it." Looking pointedly at his hands on her arms, she said, "You are the one who sought me out. Drop your hands, James."

"Drop my hands?" Jerking her hard, he shook his head. "You don't understand, do you? This isn't going to end with me saying I'm sorry and walking away. You are going to have to be punished for the things you've done."

Not going to end.

Punished for the things she'd done.

He was going to hurt her. Just like he'd hurt Lora Weaver. Just like he'd gone after Amy. Just like he'd beaten Bethany Williams two years ago.

"Why did you do this?" she whispered. "Why have you been terrorizing women? What possessed you to bring so much pain to all of us?"

"I haven't terrorized anyone. I've only been delivering consequences that the preachers or the deacons should have handed out all along. But they didn't. Preacher Eli only talked about forgiveness! Forgiveness don't mean anything, not really. Vengeance is what counts." He dropped his hands, giving her some relief . . . until he stepped closer, crowding her space.

Hardly allowing her to see anything but him.

"Someone had to do it. Ain't so? What's been going on isn't right. Women are forgetting their place. Tainting our way of life. Disrespecting our traditions."

She shook her head. She knew right then and there that she needed to speak from her heart. To voice how she felt. He wasn't going to let her go. He wasn't going to let her walk away from him.

He was going to hurt her the same way he did Lora. The same way he did the other women. He was taller. He was stronger.

She had no one nearby to help her.

She could only hope to survive. Finally, at long last, she realized that she wasn't alone, though. In fact, she never had been. God was always with her. He had directed this moment and He was the one who would help her get through it.

That knowledge gave her the strength she needed to continue. Even though she felt uncertain, she was strong. Strong enough to handle anything that came her way.

Feeling more assured, Waneta knew it was time to fight back. "Only God can deliver vengeance. You know that."

"He needed my help."

"*Nee*. He needed you to follow His word. But you have ignored him. Instead of helping others, you've been hurting. You've been doing terrible things. Shameful things."

The skin around his lips pinched and turned white. The expression in his eyes pained. It was obvious that she had struck a nerve.

Gathering her courage, Waneta said, "What does Katie think of you? She can't be proud. No wife would be proud of a husband who harms other women." Before he could answer, she said sarcastically, "Or, does she merely fear you? Did you break your vows to her, James?"

For the first time, he looked flustered. "I am keeping my vows," he said, taking hold of her arms. "I am preserving our family's honor."

She didn't even try to hide the disdain she felt for him and his convoluted reasoning. "You are doing a great many things, but you are surely not doing that."

Without warning, he tightened his grip on her arms. Shook her hard. "You will say no more!" he yelled. Eyes darting left and right, he added, "Stay silent."

Then, just as abruptly, he released her with a push.

Struggling to keep her balance, Waneta scanned the area. Though it was rarely crowded, in the past she'd always seen at least one or two other people in the vicinity. There had to be someone in the distance who she could call out to.

But the fields surrounding them were empty. And all she could see were freshly shorn fields of grass, the distinctive Kentucky-blue tinge, reminding her that she was close to home but alone.

Though she knew the Lord was with her, she yearned for someone to help her. "God, please," she begged silently. "I'm so scared." She looked around, half hoping the Lord would have made someone strong and fierce appear like a Viking of old.

Unfortunately, it didn't happen.

But she did feel His presence and His belief in her. She wasn't alone.

Standing a foot away, James was glaring into the distance, breathing hard. He seemed just as off balance as she felt. Though he was physically stronger, he wasn't without weaknesses.

It was time to help herself. Even if she failed, even if she died at his hands, at least she'd go down fighting.

She needed to take advantage of his weak moment. Kicking off her flip-flops, she turned and started to run.

She'd barely made it five steps before he grabbed her again, jerking her backward. Crying out, she pulled away and kicked his shin.

He grunted. One of his hands slipped. When she kicked him again, he shoved her shoulder while the fingers of his other hand dug in deeper.

She cried out and pushed at him as hard as she could.

James retaliated by slamming her to the ground. She fell back. Her right hand tried to temper her fall, but it was useless against the force of his shove. A bone snapped in her hand as her head hit the pavement. Bells rang in her ears as warm liquid coated the back of her head.

Pain reverberated through her body as she opened her eyes and tried to focus. Then realized he was on the ground next to her. His hand was on the collar of her dress.

The sound of ripping fabric rang in her ears.

Whether it was for her own good or because she simply had no more to give, her eyes slipped to half-mast. Her vision became blurry.

She was only aware of the heat of the dirt against her back, the smell of the earth and the grasses. The pounding in her head, the pain in her arm, and the knowledge that James Eicher was finally going to be triumphant.

He was at last going to be able to succeed with her where with everyone else he had failed. He was going to rape her. Violate her.

She was not going to be able to fight him anymore. He was too heavy. She was not strong enough. The knowledge didn't give her any peace, but the clarity did allow her to look ahead. She was simply going to have to survive it. Somehow, some way, with God's help, she was going to have to overcome this moment.

Surviving was better than dying. It had to be.

Just as her vision clouded again, a voice rang out.

"James!"

She knew that voice. She'd come to trust it—and the man it belonged to—with her entire being. "Mark?" she whispered. Though the pain was making her vision blur, she tried to focus on what was going on. Mark was running toward them, his brother just steps behind. James cursed and grabbed a handful of her hair, pulling her toward him.

She gasped.

"Move away from her!" Calvin called out.

Immediately, James released her. He scrambled to get to his feet, but he was too slow. Mark and his brother grabbed hold of him and dragged him to the side. James grunted and swung his fist as Mark and Calvin systematically worked to subdue him. Curse words flew. It happened within seconds, time seeming to stand still.

Dust and dirt flew up, coated her skin, stung her eyes. She needed to move. To get out of the way. Though she felt as if her body weighed a thousand pounds, she struggled to sit up.

Just as a third person, a woman, came to her side.

Lora Weaver.

"No, no, just stay still," she whispered. "You're badly injured."

She was also still alive.

Overcome, Waneta started crying.

Lora wrapped an arm around her. "You are safe, Waneta Cain," she whispered before pulling back to give her space. "He's not going to hurt you anymore."

Waneta was so grateful, she tried to form words. However, it was a challenge. Her mouth felt dry, her throat was bruised and felt swollen.

Brushing stray strands of hair from her face, Lora shook her head. "*Nee*, don't talk. There's no need. Everything is going to be all right now. Help is on the way."

But she had to speak. She had to say what was on her mind. She had to at least try. "Lora," she whispered. Pleased that she had been able to get that word out.

Lora leaned closer. "*Jah*? What is it, honey? What do you need?"

"To thank you for being here," she whispered before sinking into oblivion.

Chapter 29

Thursday, September 8

Mark had always thought that no moment in his life could be worse than the time he'd been forced into the back of a sheriff's cruiser and brought into his office for questioning.

He'd been wrong.

Though that had been a terrible experience, it had been about himself. He'd known that he was innocent. He'd also known that he was tough enough to be able to survive whatever happened in that interrogation room. After all, he'd survived worse things at home.

Those feelings were nothing compared to how helpless and lost he felt as he stood to one side while Deputy Beck applied pressure to Waneta's head wound and barked orders into his police radio. Lora Weaver was kneeling beside him, holding Waneta's hand and whispering to her.

Mark had no idea if Waneta could hear anything. Her eyes were still closed and her body looked limp. He was tempted to kneel next to her as well. He ached to be the one to promise her that she was safe. He wanted to be the person who could ease her fears by holding her close and reassuring her that she was no longer fighting James by herself.

But he was just as afraid that his touch wouldn't comfort her at all. She could very well flinch at it. James Eicher might have caused Waneta as much damage emotionally as he did physically. It was better to wait.

Glancing down the road, Mark watched Sheriff Brewer cuff James and lead him to his vehicle. As he watched James's smug expression, Mark let other, darker thoughts consume him. Maybe he should stand at the ready, just in case the sheriff needed some help. Mark would be only too happy to subdue him again.

Stuffing his hands in his pockets, he decided to do none of those things. The sheriff didn't need his help, and Waneta was being soothed and taken care of by Deputy Beck and Lora until the ambulance arrived.

What Mark needed to do was calm down.

If that was even possible.

As if she sensed his attention, Lora glanced at him and exhaled. He nodded, letting her know that he understood. She needed to be near Waneta for as much her sake as Waneta's. They had both been through too much to be apart.

Turning away, he saw his brother. Calvin

was bent over, his hands braced on his knees. He looked just as torn up by what had just occurred. He was still breathing hard and looked pale. Even though he'd acted so world-weary and tough, his brother looked like he was just as stunned by the latest developments as Mark was.

After checking again to make sure that Waneta didn't need anything that he could provide, Mark walked toward his brother.

"What?" Calvin asked when he got close.

"Nothing. I was only making sure you were okay."

"I'm a grown man who has been living on my own for years, Mark. Of course I'm okay."

"I know that." He was embarrassed now. "I know you probably don't care how I'm feeling, but I'm pretty shaken up. I thought we hadn't gotten here in time."

Calvin's belligerent expression cleared. "I'm pretty shaken up, too."

"It's amazing that we got here. What if we hadn't gone to the diner? What if Henry hadn't worried about Waneta walking home by herself? What if we hadn't run as fast as we did?" Mark knew he was on the verge of tears, but he didn't care. The images that were coming to mind were too upsetting.

But then Calvin reached out and gripped his arm. "Don't go there, Mark. What matters is that all those things did happen." He laughed softly. "You know what? My faith has been wavering for years, but us finding her had to have been the Lord's doing. There's no other explanation."

Mark couldn't disagree. He'd spent his day off working on the house and mowing the Cains' lawn. Then, when Calvin had shown up, they'd gone to Bill's Diner to eat. They'd been placed in Lora's section, one booth down from Deputy Beck.

The deputy's appearance had spooked Calvin. At first, he hadn't wanted to stay, but Mark held his ground. Only when he pointed out how the deputy only seemed to have eyes for Lora did Calvin settle down.

But just as they finished their meals, Lora walked toward them, a worried expression on her face. "I'm worried," she said. "Mr. Lehmann just called and said Waneta was walking home by herself because some-one had slashed the tires on her bicycle."

Mark had shaken his head. "*Nee*. She wouldn't walk home by herself. She promised me she wouldn't."

"But she did."

Exchanging a look with Calvin, Mark threw a twenty on the table and ran outside.

It had been Calvin who had suggested that they cut through two farmers' properties to get to the back road that Waneta usually walked or rode her bike on. Side by side, they'd jumped fences and ran like lightning through pastures.

That was how they'd found her just in time. Lora and Deputy Beck arrived less than five minutes later. But those five minutes had made a big difference for Waneta. Mark could hardly imagine what might have occurred if he and Calvin hadn't gotten there when they had.

"I'm real glad we found her," Calvin said, bringing Mark back to the present. "And we did find her, brother. That's all that matters."

"Thank you," Mark said.

"For what? Helping Waneta?"

"For being here. For coming back to Hart County and not leaving again. Even when I didn't want you to be here. Thank you for not giving up."

Calvin appeared to look like he was going to argue that point, but then he shook his head wearily. "You're welcome, but we both know my reasons for reaching out to you weren't good. Especially not at first."

"All that matters is that you are here now."

Mark could hear sirens in the distance. In seconds, the ambulance would arrive. Probably more police cars, too. Eventually, Waneta would go to the hospital and Sheriff Brewer or Deputy Beck would want to talk to both him and Calvin.

This rare moment between the two of them

would be gone. "What else is on your mind?" Mark asked, because Calvin kept looking at him curiously.

"You know what it is. I'm trying to wrap my head around what I just saw. I'm fairly stunned."

Mark knew Calvin wasn't speaking of James's attack. No, he was referring to how Mark had fought James. Remembering the anger that had been coursing through him made him uneasy. "Because . . . " he asked, not wanting to give anything away.

"Because you got right there on the ground and attacked James. I didn't think you had that in you."

Mark examined his brother carefully, just to be certain that Calvin wasn't pulling his leg. When he realized that he was being completely sincere, Mark didn't know whether to be offended or find humor in his reaction. "Are you really that surprised that I was defending Waneta? What did you think I would do? Ignore what was happening?"

This time Calvin looked a little shamefaced. "Probably not. But I didn't think you would attack like you did. You went at him with great, ah, vigor."

"Vigor?"

"It's an appropriate description."

"Not hardly."

"Come on. You were tough. As tough as you needed to be."

Well, he supposed that was true. Mark grinned. "I tell you what, Calvin. Only you could manage to make me feel like laughing at a time like this. Seriously, though, I'm grateful for you. And Lora. And Deputy Beck. I couldn't have helped Waneta and captured James on my own. Together, we got him."

"Now it's my turn to feel shocked," Calvin said. "You don't need to thank me. I wouldn't have wanted to be anywhere else. I'm glad I was there."

"What are you going to do now?"

All trace of humor faded from his face. "I had intended to disappear. The gang I owe money to ain't going to forget about it."

"Do you still intend to do that?" Mark hated the thought, but he knew he couldn't stop him from leaving.

Calvin shook his head. "I think I might talk to the sheriff about my options."

"Really?"

"Yeah. I know a lot of people who are in fairly high positions in a couple of gangs in the state." He shrugged. "Maybe there's a way to use that to my advantage. Then I might actually have a chance."

"I hope so."

"Me, too."

Two cruisers were now parked nearby. Mark turned and watched as Sheriff Brewer talked to the EMTs, knelt down to say something to Waneta, who was now awake, then directed the deputy to put James in the back of one of the vehicles.

Then the sheriff turned to Mark and motioned for him to approach.

"Looks like you're on," Calvin said.

"Yeah. Wish me luck."

"You don't need it, Mark. You are the hero today."

That statement was ringing in his ears as he resolutely walked toward Sheriff Brewer. "Sheriff."

Sheriff Brewer held out his hand. "I just talked to Eddie. As you know, he used to be an EMT. He thinks Waneta is going to be okay."

Mark exhaled. "Do you know if anyone went to go fetch her parents?"

"Lora thinks one of the servers at the diner went to go get them."

Feeling relieved, he took a deep breath. "Waneta will be glad about that."

"Now that she's awake, I know you probably want to go sit with her, but can you tell me what happened?"

As Calvin joined them, Mark quickly relayed Lora's announcement at the diner and what he and Calvin had decided to do. He briefly described their fight and how Deputy Beck was able to take over the moment he arrived on the scene.

Sheriff Brewer looked from one of them to the other. "You spending time together now?"

Just as Mark nodded, Calvin said, "Yeah." Then he gestured to the two officers standing next to the vehicle where James was sitting. "What's going to happen to him?"

Sheriff Brewer pursed his lips. "Justice," he said after a pause.

As Mark walked back to Waneta's side, he breathed a sigh of relief. No woman in Hart County was going to be in danger anymore.

At least not from James Eicher.

Chapter 30

After Waneta had regained consciousness, Lora moved to the side. Deputy Beck and the EMTs had taken Waneta's vitals, started an IV, and loaded her into the ambulance.

After the sheriff spoke with Mark and Calvin, he and another officer left the scene.

Soon after the ambulance workers arrived, Mr. and Mrs. Cain showed up. Bill and Mia had obviously left the diner and picked them up.

As they took in the scene and spoke to one of the policemen, their eyes had filled with tears. They'd approached the ambulance with shaky steps, the policeman hovering over them.

Mark had stepped out of the ambulance and hugged them both before guiding them to a spot where they could speak to her. Then, as if he couldn't bear to be separated from Waneta any longer, he'd climbed back into the ambulance just before it headed to the hospital, lights flashing.

It was obvious Mark and Waneta were a strong

couple now. Mark had saved her today, but she had saved him weeks ago when she offered him trust and her friendship. No longer would either of them have to walk through life alone.

Lora hadn't been standing by herself the whole time. Calvin had lingered for a while. He'd even spoken a couple of words to her, but it was obvious that neither of them was comfortable around the other anymore. After mumbling something about being glad everyone was all right, he darted off.

Soon, the other vehicles left.

Now only she and Deputy Beck lingered.

Well, actually, he wasn't there lingering at all. He'd been busy taking samples of dirt and grass. Every so often he would bend down on one knee, peer at something more closely, then put it into a plastic bag.

He'd also darted curious looks her way several times.

She'd been tempted to offer to help, but she knew it was police business. She was also a little afraid that if she broke the silence, he would ask her to leave. She didn't want to do that.

Finally he straightened, put the last of the dirt samples in an envelope, and walked over.

"I'm about done here. Do you want a ride?"

She did, but she was suddenly feeling awkward around him. He had to have a lot to do, and she would just be in the way. "I'll be okay.

315

It's only a ten-minute walk for me from here."

"Are you sure? My truck has air-conditioning, though it probably won't cool off until I pull into the station's parking lot."

Huh. It seemed he was feeling just as tentative as she was. Just an hour ago, she'd hopped into his truck when he'd torn out of the diner parking lot.

Feeling a little amused by how they were acting, she raised her eyebrows. "So you're asking me to sit in a hot truck with you?"

"I am, but what I'm really asking is if we could spend some time together."

Her pulse jumped. She wanted to hope. Wanted it so badly, especially after he'd stayed at her side for hours in the hospital.

However, he'd distanced himself since then. He'd called her, but their conversations had centered on her health. He hadn't asked if he could stop by her house. And today was the first time in a week that he'd gone out to eat at the diner when she was working.

Common sense told her that he was busy, trying to locate James and see to his other responsibilities. But there was another part of her that feared that he'd simply grown tired of her. She'd misjudged far too many people for most of her life to expect too much from him.

That was why she looked at him curiously.

"Do you have some questions for me about James?"

"Nope."

"Oh. Well, then . . . "

After a moment, he smiled. "Lora, are you really going to make me say it?"

Say what? "I'm afraid I am. I have no idea what's on your mind."

"Really?"

"You ain't making things any easier, Deputy Beck."

"Eddie. You called me Eddie on our date. Remember?"

Biting her bottom lip, she nodded.

"And before you start questioning anything else, I'm just going to say the words. I like you. I want to get to know you better."

Staring into his eyes, Lora wished for a lot of things. She wished she was a whole lot more accomplished and a whole lot more innocent. She wished they'd met another way and that he hadn't had to investigate her.

But most of all, she wished that she was confident enough to believe that none of those things mattered.

"I like you, too. But do you really think something between us could work out?"

He pulled his ball cap off his head, then put it back on, this time backward, with the bill at his back. "I do. Why don't you?"

She could see his eyes better now. He looked sincere. She knew he was sincere. But that didn't mean she trusted a future with the two of them together. "You know why," hating that she was stating the obvious. "We're pretty different."

"Yeah, we are." He grinned. "I don't have pretty, long blond hair and legs that go on forever."

She was pleased he thought she was pretty, but she needed to know that they had something more than that. "You know what I mean."

"Would you believe me if I said I don't care that we're really different?"

"I would believe you, but I'd also say that you're being naïve. Our differences are going to matter one day, Eddie. To you, and also to your friends and your family."

"Before I accept what you're saying and leave you alone, let me ask you one thing . . . Are you done?"

Done? "I don't understand what you're asking."

"You've already accomplished a lot. You got your GED. You have a good job and people like you there. You've had the courage to return to Horse Cave even when you knew coming back wouldn't be easy. You survived a brutal attack, and you were brave enough to help Waneta. Could you have done all that two years ago?"

"*Nee*." Two years ago she'd been living with a jerk and trying to save up enough money to go out on her own.

"So you're different than you used to be." Slowly, he smiled. "That's why I'm asking you, are you done growing and changing?"

"No."

"I'm not done, either. That's why I don't want you to start telling me about all the ways we are different, because we are going to be different people next year. Maybe even next month."

His reasoning was a bit optimistic. But then she remembered Mark Fisher. He'd been accused of beating a woman, then practically shunned. What if he'd given up?

She knew that answer. He'd still be struggling like Calvin was. And what a waste that would have been. "You know what? I think I would like that ride, Eddie."

His gaze warmed. "My reasons swayed you, then?"

A lot of things did. Hopes and dreams swayed her. But she didn't think he needed to know that. "Yep. You are a very persuasive man."

"Good." Glancing at his phone, he said, "Let me take you home, then I've got to get back to work."

It was time to take a chance. "You know, I'm not working tonight. And I don't just work in a diner. I can cook pretty good, too. Would you like to come over for supper?"

"It might be late. Close to seven."

"It might not be fancy, just a casserole with two sides."

Opening the passenger door for her, he nodded. "I'd like that."

She left the door open while he walked around because the inside of the vehicle was really hot. But after everything that had just happened, it didn't matter to her at all.

Chapter 31

Thursday, September 15

Sharing a bemused look with her mother, Waneta inspected the small olive tree beside the couch, which Mr. Lehmann had sent over. "This is mighty nice. I don't believe I've ever seen an olive tree before."

"Me, neither. It's pretty with its silver leaves. It will look mighty nice in the garden."

"And in the kitchen in the winter, since Henry said that it can't take the cold."

Her mother fingered the leaves. "No offense to your boss, but this is a strange sort of gift, don't you think? He gave you a tree that bears olives, which you don't eat; and it requires a lot of time and attention, which you don't have to give."

Waneta had just been thinking the same thing. "I don't understand it, either, but maybe one day I will."

"That's the spirit, dear. Yes, indeed, one day you'll understand why you have an olive tree."

"You girls worry too much about things that ain't important," Daed said. "All that matters is that Waneta is safe and sound."

"She's safe, but I don't know about sound. She still has a broken wrist and more bumps, cuts, and bruises on her than any girl should ever have."

"I'm going to be okay, Mamm," Waneta said softly. Just as she had for the last week.

Her mother resituated the pillow under her cast. "I hope so."

"I know so. Now, please stop worrying so much. You heard what the doctors said. I need to rest for two weeks, but then I can go back to work, at least part-time."

"I'm going to make sure you do rest, daughter," Daed said as he got up to answer the knock at the door. "And I'm going to make sure your visitor knows not to get you too riled up as well."

Curious as to who could be visiting now, Waneta watched her father open the door in an almost spry manner. If there was a silver lining to all that had occurred, that had to be it, she surmised. Her father was moving around better than he had in years. It seemed he liked being as needed as she did.

"Ah, now. Look who has returned," Daed said. "Mark."

Staring at him, Waneta felt her cheeks heat. "I didn't know you were planning to stop by today."

"I wanted it to be a surprise," he said.

"Really?" She wondered why. He had to know how much she liked being around him and it was obvious that her parents adored him.

"We were all just admiring Waneta's new olive tree," Mamm said.

Walking over, Mark knelt on the floor next to the couch and smiled. "I told Henry that flowers might be just as appreciated, but he was fixated on this olive tree. He said olive trees symbolize good fortune and prosperity."

"In that case, I'll try even harder to take good care of it," she joked.

"I'm sure you will." Turning to her, he reached out and ran his thumb along her cheek. "Now, how are you doing today?"

His voice was low and sweet. And his touch? Well, she couldn't deny that she liked his attentions. "Better now," she whispered.

Tracing the line of her eyebrow, he said, "Sure?"

Hardly aware of anything but his loving glance and touch, she nodded.

"We are going to go outside!" Mamm announced from behind them. "You know what? We might even go for a little walk."

"A long one," Daed said. "So don't you worry about us."

Mark's lips twitched as her parents bustled out the door. "They are two of a kind, your parents."

"Indeed. They're the best kind, though. They have been so wonderful these last couple of days."

"Good." Rubbing her cheek, he focused on her

again. She felt his gaze traipse from her hairline to her cheek to the cast on her wrist. "Waneta, I don't know what I would have done if you hadn't survived."

"We won't ever have to know. You and Calvin got there in time."

Releasing a ragged sigh, he nodded. "I know you're right. I keep hoping if I tell myself that long enough, I might even believe it." After climbing to his feet, he looked down at her. "Any chance you have enough room on this couch for two?"

"There's plenty of room, if you don't mind my feet on your lap."

"How about I hold your head in my lap instead? I've got some things I want to talk to you about."

Since she didn't care where he was, as long as he was close, she simply smiled. Then laughed as Mark tried to resituate her without harming her ribs, head, or arm. When he had at last repositioned her to his liking, she stared up at his handsome face. "What did you want to talk to me about?"

"I've got some updates for you. First of all, it seems my brother has nine lives. He talked his way into some kind of situation with some kind of government agency. He's going to do some undercover work for them."

"What does that mean? Where will he be? Do you think that's safe?"

"To answer your questions, I don't know, I don't know, and finally, I don't know." Smiling at her look of surprise, he shrugged. "I'm okay with not knowing and you should be, too."

"Really? Why?"

"Because at least we'll know he's on the straight and narrow and alive. That's a positive thing."

Relaxing against him, she nodded. "You're right. I'm glad for Calvin."

Running a hand up and down her good arm, he continued. "Now, are you ready for the second piece of news?"

"*Jah.*"

"You sure? It's big."

"I'm lying down. I should be able to handle it."

"All right, then, but brace yourself."

"Mark! What is it?"

"Lora and Deputy Beck eloped last night."

She gaped. "Surely not."

"Oh, *jah.*" He chuckled. "She called the store to tell me so no one would worry when she wasn't around for the next week." Looking pleased as punch, he said, "Right now, they are on their honeymoon in Gatlinburg."

"I'm amazed. But I kind of think it's fitting, too. Lora never was the type to play by the rules."

"For what it's worth, she sounded really happy."

"That's worth a lot. I'm glad for her." Waneta still felt bad whenever she thought about how she never really did have much to do with Lora. That was going to change, though. They'd been through far too much to go back to being distant acquaintances.

Smiling up at him, she sighed. "I'm real glad you came over, Mark. You are filled with good news."

"I'm not done yet." Looking a little awkward, he said, "I have one more thing to share."

"Really? Who is this bit of news about? Henry?"

The smile vanished. "No. Me."

"You?" she teased, then tensed. "Wait a minute. Did something happen?" All kinds of worst-case scenarios came to mind. "Is Sheriff Brewer mad at you? Or did something go wrong with your job? Or your house?"

Grinning, he shook his head. "The answer is no. Four times."

"Mark, don't play games."

"All right, then. Here's my news, Waneta. I've fallen in love with you."

"Oh!"

"Yeah, oh. And since I have fallen in love, I decided I had better talk to you about that."

She felt like laughing and crying. "What . . . What did you want to talk about?"

"Well, first, I'm going to have to ask you not to keep me in suspense. Do you love me, too?"

"You know I do."

Raising her hand, he kissed her knuckles. "*Jah.*

326

I do know you do. You were there for me when practically no one else was. You've defended me when most didn't think I deserved it. You've taught me to trust again. To believe again."

"I don't know if I did all those things, but I do know that I'm better with you, Mark Fisher."

Leaning down, he brushed his lips against her forehead. "Now, I have something to ask you, and I want you to think about it long and hard before you answer."

She pretended to brace herself. "All right. I'm ready."

"Will you marry me, Waneta Cain?"

She didn't need to consider it. She sure didn't need any more time to pass. "Yes."

He sighed dramatically. "You just promised me that you'd think on this for a while."

She was injured. She was so weak and sore that she was lying with her head in his lap instead of sitting by his side. She was also younger than him. And far shyer than he'd ever been.

But there was one area where she was far and away his superior.

And that was believing in the two of them.

"I just promised to marry you, Mark Fisher. That trumps everything else."

"Does it, now?"

"Very much so. And that means, it's time for you to do one thing."

"Which is?"

Looking into his eyes, she smiled. "Kiss me."

Next thing she knew, Waneta was sitting in his lap. Her arms were looped around his neck. He was holding her with care . . . and kissing her like he didn't intend to stop anytime soon.

As she relaxed against him, Waneta sincerely hoped that was the case.

After all, they had a lifetime of happiness to look forward to.

Center Point Large Print
600 Brooks Road / PO Box 1
Thorndike, ME 04986-0001 USA

(207) 568-3717

US & Canada:
1 800 929-9108
www.centerpointlargeprint.com